ENDORSEMENTS

"I highly recommend every American read The Engineered Downfall of America, which clearly documents the forces that have stealthily been at work to create crises, setting the stage for a dictator. . . If enough Americans can read Michael Cordner's excellent book, there is hope! Forewarned is forearmed!"

(WILLIAM J. FEDERER, BEST-SELLING AUTHOR OF OVER TWENTY BOOKS, INCLUDING AMERICA'S GOD AND COUNTRY: ENCYCLOPEDIA OF QUOTATIONS.)

"*The Engineered Downfall of America* combines a vital analysis of the historical basis for America's greatness with the challenge to serious Christians and the church to ongoing prayer for returning the nation to its biblical foundations."

(JOHN STORMER, BEST-SELLING AUTHOR OF NONE DARE CALL IT TREASON, THE DEATH OF A NATION, BETRAYED BY THE BENCH, AND NONE DARE CALL IT EDUCATION.)

"*The Engineered Downfall of America* is very well written and explains the general situation admirably. . . It has exactly captured the situation we are in."

(J. R. NYQUIST, WELL-KNOWN GEOPOLITICAL ANALYST AND AUTHOR OF ORIGINS OF THE FOURTH WORLD WAR, AND CO-AUTHOR OF THE NEW TACTICS OF GLOBAL WAR.)

THE
ENGINEERED DOWNFALL
OF AMERICA

How It Happened and Where We Can Find Hope

MICHAEL CORDNER

THE
ENGINEERED DOWNFALL
OF AMERICA

Copyright © 2016 by Michael Cordner

World Ahead Press is a division of WND Books. The views and opinions expressed in this book are those of the author and do not necessarily reflect the official policy or position or WND Books.

Paperback ISBN: 978-1-944212-40-7
eBook ISBN: 978-1-944212-41-4

Printed in the United States of America
16 17 18 19 20 21 LSI 9 8 7 6 5 4 3 2 1

DEDICATION

Dedicated to my grandchildren,
with loving prayers for their future.

CONTENTS

FOREWORD

I s Communism dead? Michael Cordner, the author of this book, says it isn't dead. And Michael Cordner is right. Not only is Communism alive and well on American college campuses, it is alive and well throughout the world. In fact, the ruling party in China is Communist; and China is the world's most populous country. The ruling party in Russia is Communist in all but name, and Russia is the world's largest country. Since the supposed fall of the Communist Bloc many countries have been taken over by the Communists. South Africa, for example, is ruled by the African National Congress which is controlled by the South African Communist Party. In 1999, Hugo Chavez, a stealth Communist supported by Fidel Castro, became president of Venezuela—a country that is now a Cuban colony. In 1997 the Communists took over Congo. In 2002, after 27 years of fighting, the Communists won the civil war in Angola. In 2008 the Communists took over Nepal. In Brazil, the Workers' Party won power by pretending to be "moderate," but in truth was led by pro-Moscow Communists working with Fidel Castro and the Colombian terrorists known as the FARC (Revolutionary Armed Forces of Colombia). In Nicaragua a Marxist Leninist Party—the Sandinistas—returned to power in 2007.

But nobody noticed—especially American conservatives. After all, they wanted to claim that Ronald Reagan defeated Communism in the Cold War. Yet, in Eastern Europe, where Communism supposedly disappeared, we find the ruling families of the old Communist system in control of major corporations, government ministries, banks, and major media outlets. In former Soviet Ukraine, where the people were supposedly freed from Communism in 1991, a revolution took place in which hundreds of statues of Lenin were torn down in 2014. But wait a minute! Why were those statues still standing twenty-three years after the supposed collapse of the Soviet Union? Even more telling, when Moscow's puppet president in Ukraine was toppled from power that same year, the Kremlin reacted by invading and annexing Crimea, as well as triggering a civil war in Eastern Ukraine. Some Ukrainians who understood the inner workings of the former Soviet Union at the time stated that Ukraine's revolution was directed against the Communist Party Soviet Union—which had gone underground in 1991, and secretly held power in Russia as well as Ukraine.

Across the globe, in country after country, the Communists continued in power while denying they were Communists. Even when their parties carried an ostensible Communist label they denied that the label had any meaning. There are even politicians, here in the United States, claiming to be "Democrats" who are quite obviously Marxists. The universal phenomenon of our time is the Communist who denies he is a Communist. Yet it is Communism, again and again, that continues to advance. One only has to look at the gradual and ongoing transformation of the United States itself, or the Eurozone. It is not only Latin America that is being taken over by Communists masquerading as "moderate leftists." It is not only in Africa, or in Nepal, where the Communists continue to win victory after victory. Yet statesmen from around the world insist on the fiction that Communist China is a capitalist country. It's as if all the Communists on Earth, working out of the same play book, changed their stripes on cue. Yet, if you were paying close attention, this magic trick was not so magic after all. In December 2000, when Putin first visited Communist Cuba, a journalist asked Putin if he was a Communist. The Russian president answered cryptically, "Call me a pot but heat me not."

Do you really want to know if Communism is dead? Let me warn you. It is inconvenient to know the truth. It is unpleasant. If you give Michael Cordner's book the time of day you will find yourself squirming. "No," you say to yourself, "this isn't true." You heard a few misleading quotes on television, and saw a few camera shots. You believed the Russian lies. You believed that nice politician on TV. You never understood the enemy of your country. You never understood the subversives who were burning American flags in the 1960s. You never realized that Marxism was infiltrating your church, your local city council, your school board. Did you notice when they started electing closet Communists to the White House? Think back, and do not lie to yourself; for it was Joseph McCarthy who was "blacklisted by history" and not the Communists. Their crimes were admitted of course, but the Communists themselves disappeared. They were transformed into "Democrats"—in Russia, in Brazil, in the United States and Europe.

When Michael Cordner says that America "is now under far greater control from the radical left than it has ever been," he is not exaggerating. He is telling you an essential fact. He is describing an iceberg that has already struck our ship of state. But most of us weren't paying attention. We were fast asleep, and we still are. The Communist victories listed above took place in plain sight. They took place after the supposed collapse of Communism. Now ask yourself how that is possible. A thing cannot collapse and continue to expand. No, it cannot happen that way—unless the collapse itself was a ruse. But you shake your head. You do not believe in ruses because you do not understand Communist tactics. You never understood the subject of Communism. To be honest, you never really studied it. Well, here's your chance. Perhaps it is your last chance.

Today the situation is more and more obvious. Russia has been building new tanks, submarines and missiles. China is doing the same. Meanwhile, the United States has been spontaneously disarming. Look at the headlines. Read the newspapers. There are stories appearing every week about the deteriorating state of the US Navy, the Air Force and the Army. If you want to understand the conflict that is approaching from afar, then you will have to take another look at Communism. On this subject Michael Cordner's book is a good place to start. Here is outlined the basics, the fundamental facts and much-needed context in a language that anyone can understand.

At this late hour, after so many years of willful ignorance, it is easier than ever to show that America has been subverted, infiltrated, betrayed and outmaneuvered during the past half century. Yet most Americans are oblivious— and this is shameful. How will our people cope, and how will they survive the disasters that follow from ignorance? I am sad to say that our posterity—if we have a posterity at all—will judge us very harshly. To have inherited the greatest nation in history, and to have lost it by such far-reaching stupidity and dereliction of duty, is almost unprecedented. Therefore, if you are a serious person, if you are a person who loves his country, this book is for you.

J. R. Nyquist
Eureka California, 26 April 2016

ACKNOWLEDGMENTS

The material in this book draws much from the work of others, particularly from books by John Stormer, Phyllis Schlafly and Chester Ward (writing jointly), Roger Kimball, and lectures given by Dr. James Bowers.

PREFACE

Many are asking what is happening to America, and why? Although we supposedly won the Cold War, we are now deep into the process of losing our liberty and the traditional American way of life—the very things we thought had been secured in winning that war! Simply put, our republic is falling apart. We find ourselves in the final stages of a complete cultural makeover that has radically transformed our society, including the philosophy and operation of government and the purpose of its laws. Old-fashioned American values and patriotism have been replaced by egalitarianism and socialist ideals, and their destructive effect is cumulative. Our leaders, and the fundamental institutions that operate society now have no regard for the Christian values and principles upon which our nation was founded and upon which our liberty was based. We are heading toward the worst economic collapse and break down of society we have ever seen, and in the ensuring chaos the federal government will take complete control of everything. Our enemies, who are aggressively building their arms while we reduce ours, will take advantage of our state and all-out war will come to our shores. People at present cannot see or accept this, and when these things begin to happen there will be an absolute state of shock and disbelief, with no idea how we ever got to such a point.

To understand the present and prepare for the future we have to know something of the past. As such, a major purpose of this book is to document how America was betrayed and transformed during the Cold War period, setting the stage for what is now happening to our country. Knowing this will make our nation's present state more understandable and the future we are rushing into very believable. The other major purpose of this book is to address the real underlying reason *why* we are in this present state, and that in spite of it, there can still be hope for the future.

Most Americans have little or no idea how deeply our nation was penetrated and manipulated by Marxists during the Cold War. They will have difficulty with this and their response will be, "This is America, that couldn't happen here!" *But it did*, and what follows will document exactly how and by whom, up to our present day.

The political betrayal of our nation during the Cold War period opened wide the door for present-day betrayers to become even more deeply entrenched in the fabric of our nation. And the Cultural Revolution of the 1960s and 70s transformed our society by annihilating its Judeo-Christian values, thus doing away with the yardstick of truth by which all things should be measured and evaluated. This has devastated the process of logical thinking, and the public has become so blind that they sleepwalk to the polling booths and vote for those who are openly destroying our nation, our liberty and everything we have stood for. Their blindness is such that the new breed of betrayers no longer have to bother too much about hiding what is really happening. Look briefly at the following examples of what is being done as they lead our nation to ruin.

Look at our economy, how the fundamental principles of economics we all have to live by in our private lives and business endeavors if we are to stay afloat are being violated. Look at what is happening to the whole political process, the blatant lying, deception, and corruption that spews out of the daily news. Look at what is being done to our military strength and preparedness. Look at how we have betrayed our friends and allies, and demeaned the integrity, reputation, and respect of our nation before the whole world.

And look at how we bow, scrape and fawn over those who call us "the great Satan" and vow to bring us down. No matter—we do all we can to accommodate them, refusing to connect what they say and do with their religion, even though they openly claim and prove it is their sacred writings that drive them. We protect their religious sensibilities to the point of absurdity—like flat-out refusing to call Muslim terrorists "Muslim terrorists!" We are far more concerned with their rights and feelings than with those of the Christians who are being exterminated in Middle East countries under Islamic rule. Far more!

Why are we letting them do all this to our country, what is wrong with us? *Are we all asleep?* This is *our* country, *not theirs!* What they are doing is out in the open, nothing conspiratorial about it! Anyone who doesn't see it doesn't want to see it, or they have been so indoctrinated and educated out of their common sense they simply *cannot* see it, which now includes the majority of the voting public.

While most of us are aware of the threats posed by radical Islam, and we see what Muslim immigrants are doing to the European Union, most Americans are still in denial over Communism. The end of the Cold War supposedly took care of that. But in a very real sense, the Cold War did *not* end. It changed its form and the way it was fought, but the epic struggle between two radically different ideologies for the control of society and nations did not cease. While the collapse of the Soviet Union was a very significant set-back for the cause of international Communism, the cause itself did not go away. Communist leaders back then did not just give up. In fact, most of them were still in political power right after the collapse. They changed their political label and cleaned up their act, but not their hardcore Communist mentality and drive.

Consider that an estimated 100 million people have been murdered under Communism. Communist leaders who perpetrated, supported and could justify such atrocities *had to be totally committed to the cause of worldwide Communism.* They were not about to throw in the towel and quit! They went underground to come back when the time was right, when America and the West would be occupied elsewhere, weakened and consumed with their own problems. The struggle went to a far more dangerous level as America and the West dropped their guard. (Enemy? What enemy?)

Now, some twenty-six years after the announced end of the Cold War, we see their return. Russia is reestablishing a full-blown Soviet-style government, with a relentless, massive arms build-up, and a return to naked political and military aggression. The cause is openly moving forward under the very able leadership of a former Cold War KGB colonel (Vladimir Putin), and it is reported by a former high-level Soviet bloc official that more than half of those in his government are former Cold War KGB officers.[1]

Add to this the fact that America is now under far greater control from the radical left than it has ever been. And Muslims are adopting similar tactics of penetration, manipulation and naked aggression to establish their do-or-die goal of a world-wide caliphate, which necessitates first bringing America down.

Welcome to the real world!

CHAPTER 1

BEGINNINGS

THE RADICAL LEFT BEGINS ITS INFLUX

We need to go back to where the political and social philosophies that have led to America's present state really got a foothold.

The early part of the twentieth century saw the introduction of the "Progressive Era," and the idea that big government was the way to solve our problems. Supposedly, the country could be run with greater efficiency, uniformity and fairness under centralized control, so big government was seen as the best way to solve our problems. Many universities became left-wing in their ideology and teaching. Socialist and Marxist professors and administrators began to fill key positions. By the 1930s, America's most prestigious schools had been infiltrated with Marxist ideas and teaching (although usually not under that name). Upholding Judeo-Christian principles and values and the free-market ideal that made this country great became passé. With the increasing rejection of biblical morality and principles of government, the existence of absolute truth (a fixed moral compass) was ridiculed and rejected.

Courses began to teach that the problems of society stem from capitalism (described as the exercise of "unrestrained greed") and the rigid inflexibility of Christian morality. Students learned that Socialism and the flexibility of relative morality is the wave of the future. They were skillfully manipulated into becoming anti-Christian, anti-capitalist, and anti-American. They tacitly became Socialist and pro-Marxist in ideology, believing that anything that advanced these ideals was morally right. Students who did not have a solid traditional Christian foundation and reference point for evaluating what they were taught were easily taken in. Top grades and honors went to those who were the most thoroughly indoctrinated, and on graduation they were snapped up by organizations who were looking to hire the very best—notably in education, the media, and government. Thus, a new breed of educators, news broadcasters and analysts, politicians, diplomats and government bureaucrats came into being who had been educated to reject America's traditional Christian, Capitalist values, and accept humanistic morals and Socialist ideals.

Marxist philosophy first had a significant impact on American domestic policy under President Roosevelt in the 1930s. His collectivist policies could not be labeled Socialism (the American public would not accept that), so they were given a very innocuous label—the "New Deal." While Roosevelt was not a professing Marxist, his economic advisors most certainly were. They were known as the "Roosevelt Brain Trust" who were the architects of the New Deal and its Social Security system. Their leader was Rexford Tugwell, head of the Economics Department at Columbia University, who so admired Soviet Communism his nickname was Red Rex. He had visited The Soviet Union with a large group of trade unionists, economists, intellectuals and businessmen in 1927. They were given the grand tour, shown the "prospering" economy, and spent six hours talking with Joseph Stalin.

In 1930, Tugwell co-authored a book, *American Economic Life and the Means of Its Improvement*. Although he admitted having problems with certain dictatorial aspects of their system, he had nothing but praise for Soviet Communism, believing it would be more prosperous and egalitarian than capitalism.[1] He represented the brains behind Roosevelt's policies, and was one of his closest confidants and advisors.

THE FALL OF EASTERN EUROPE TO COMMUNISM (1944)

The fall of Eastern Europe to Soviet control at the end of WW II was tragic, and certainly not inevitable. It could be attributed in a major way to President Roosevelt's apparent blindness concerning the true nature of Communism, and his unreasoned trust in Soviet leader Joseph Stalin. Roosevelt had been supportive of the Soviet Union from the beginning of his presidency. He granted them diplomatic recognition in 1933, despite information given to him by the US State Department strongly warning him of their revolutionary aims and practices and advising against recognition. Roosevelt felt that Stalin was simply misunderstood by the West, and went ahead anyway.

The fate of post-war Europe was primarily determined at the Yalta Conference in 1944, attended by the United States, the Soviet Union and Great Britain, in which Roosevelt was not at all averse to letting Stalin have his way in Eastern Europe. US diplomat and Soviet specialist Charles Bohlen was Roosevelt's Russian interpreter at that conference, and he gives an account of Roosevelt's beliefs about Stalin in his memoirs. "President Roosevelt felt that Stalin viewed the world somewhat in the same light as he did, and that Stalin's hostility and distrust, which were evident in wartime conferences, were due to the neglect that Soviet Russia had suffered at the hands of other countries for years after the Revolution." Roosevelt did not understand that there was a profound ideological difference between them.[2]

George Keenan, another Russian-speaking American diplomat in the US Foreign Service during Roosevelt's presidency, recalls in his book that Roosevelt believed that at base, Stalin was just like everyone else. He had been bluntly rejected by the "arrogant conservatives" in Western capitals. Roosevelt believed that the Russian cooperation with the West could be obtained "if only Stalin was exposed to the charm of a personality of FDR's caliber. There were no grounds at all for this assumption; it was so childish that it was really unworthy of a statesman of FDR's standing."[3]

Bohlen's memoirs describe how there had been a "quiet struggle in the [Roosevelt] administration against the soupy and syrupy attitude toward the Soviet Union." And America's first ambassador to the Soviet Union in 1933, William C. Bullitt, never missed an opportunity to warn Roosevelt of Stalin's treachery, to which he would reply:

> *Bill, I don't dispute your facts; they are accurate. I don't dispute the logic of your reasoning. I just have a hunch that Stalin is not that kind of man. Harry [Hopkins] says he's not and that he doesn't want anything but security for his country, and I think if I give him everything I possibly can and ask for nothing in return, noblesse oblige, he won't try to annex anything and will work with me for a world of democracy and peace.[4]*

So Roosevelt, who really had the final say over Churchill in leading the West, had no problem with trusting Stalin and giving him anything he wanted, including the fate of Eastern Europe. However, as we all know, Stalin *was* the kind of man Roosevelt had been warned about, who had not the slightest intention of working "for a world of democracy and peace." That should have been unquestionably obvious to all, but the door had been opened for Stalin to move in and take complete control. The post-war fate of Eastern Europe under Communism had been sealed.

Shortly after the Yalta Conference, America's ambassador to the Soviet Union, Averell Harriman, cabled Roosevelt that "we must come clearly to realize that the Soviet program is the establishment of totalitarianism, ending personal liberty and democracy as we know it." Two days later, Roosevelt began to admit he had been "excessively optimistic" and that Averell was right. [5] At last, he started to wake up, but it was too late—the damage had been done. Roosevelt died shortly after this, just months after the fateful Yalta Conference.

The Eastern European countries that had suffered so much under German and Soviet occupation had believed that America would ensure their liberty after the war. After all, America was the champion of liberty! When they were handed over to absolute totalitarian oppression under Stalin, they felt utterly betrayed (and they were!). Arthur Bliss Lane, American ambassador to Poland, resigned his post in protest, and in his book, *I Saw Poland Betrayed: An American Ambassador Reports to the American People* (1948), he describes the betrayal of Poland and Eastern Europe by US and British diplomatic leadership.

> *Our policy of appeasement toward Soviet Russia undoubtedly emboldened Stalin to go ahead with his plans for the complete domination of Poland, as of all other countries in Eastern Europe* [6]

BIRTH OF THE COLD WAR ERA AND THE UN

The term *Cold War* describes the state of political tension and military rivalry between the United States and the Soviet Union, which came short of open warfare between them. It began in 1946, and ended in 1991 with the collapse of the Soviet Union. After the war, the nations of the world fell into three camps –

1. The "Free World" – led by the United States
2. The "Communist Bloc" – led by the Soviet Union, and;
3. The "Third-World Nations" – emerging nations of Africa, Asia and South America.

To counter the threat of Communist expansion, America, Canada and ten Western European nations formed NATO (North Atlantic Treaty Organization). The Soviet Union formed a counter-alliance of Eastern European nations (the Warsaw Pact).

The United Nations (UN) was formed after the end of World War II to be the World's peace-keeper. A high US State Department official, Alger Hiss, was a key organizer of the UN and its founding Secretary General. He was later exposed as a long-time Soviet agent. A collectivist-Marxist philosophy has been at the heart of the UN since the very beginning. Every Secretary-General of the UN has been an avowed Socialist of some kind. The organization has been, and still is, diametrically opposed to the American ideal of liberty and free-enterprise. It either advances, or does nothing to prevent, the advancement of international

Communism and Socialism. As a peace-keeping force, the UN has been a total failure.

PENETRATION OF THE US STATE DEPARTMENT

To understand how America was betrayed during the Cold War era, it is necessary to understand how the US State Department was penetrated and came to be controlled by those who had a Socialist / Marxist worldview, and by outright Marxists and Soviet agents, who supported the expansion of international Communism.

Well-known veteran journalist, educator and author, M. Stanton Evans, has substantiated this in several books and articles. In a 1997 article published by Human Events magazine, Evans recounts that around 1944 a fierce internal power struggle began within the State Department in which hardline anti-Communists were ousted and replaced with hardline Socialist–Marxists.[7] This turn-over in power was completed in 1947 when General George C. Marshall became Secretary of State, with Dean Acheson second in command. In an exclusive 2007 interview with Human Events magazine editors, Evans told of the grave concern of FBI Director J. Edgar Hoover over the increasing security risks in our government, "Hoover sent report after report after report to the White House, the Attorney General, the State Department, and the Treasury Department. These reports were ignored . . . These people were all over the place and almost nothing was done about them, and quite often they were promoted and given more responsibilities."[8]

Several members of Congress became greatly alarmed over the State Department's glaring lack of concern for the threat posed to America's security by the penetration of Soviet agents. Members of the Senate Appropriations Committee sent a confidential report in June 1947 to Secretary of State George Marshall, "It is evident that there is a deliberate, calculated program being carried out not only to protect Communist personnel in high places, but to reduce security and intelligence protection to a nullity." They made reference to the FBI report on Soviet espionage involving large numbers of State Department employees which had been challenged and ignored by the State Department with the "apparent tacit approval of Mr. Acheson."[9]

Their alarmed concern fell on deaf ears. Nothing changed. In fact, things were to become much worse, as the State Department, now under pro-Communist control, further promoted the very things which so concerned these congressmen.

The Amerasia Affair

Amerasia was a journal on Far Eastern affairs, founded in 1937 by American Communists. In 1945 *Amerasia* published what the Office of Strategic Services

(OSS) recognized as a top secret government document. The offices of *Amerasia* were raided, and FBI agents arrested six people, including three US government officials, and took possession of over one thousand stolen classified documents. The highest level government employee arrested was John S. Service, a State Department official who was a senior diplomat in China. Among the confiscated documents were military reports giving secret information on the position and disposition of the Chinese nationalist army under General Chiang Kai-shek (who was fighting communist general Mao Tse-tung to prevent a communist take-over of China).

FBI director Hoover believed he had an airtight case of immense proportions in which every type of security had been breached as a federal crime, namely, theft of top-secret documents, policy subversion, perjury, cover-up and the obstruction of justice. Justice Department officials appeared ready to prosecute. However, they suddenly and inexplicably changed their tune, and the whole matter was swept under the rug. Some of the defendants were fined and the others walked away scot-free, including John Service, who returned to his State Department duties.[10]

Senator Joseph McCarthy

The extent of the problem was revealed by Wisconsin Senator Joseph McCarthy in 1950. Based on information provided by the FBI, he publically claimed that fifty people were working at various government levels who were, or had been, associated with known Communists and the American Communist Party, and were therefore high security risks. A special subcommittee was appointed, chaired by Senator Millard Tydings (D-MD) to investigate the charges. McCarthy's chief exhibit was the shocking government cover-up of the blatant security breaches in the *Amerasia* affair. However, after examining the evidence, and hearing from witnesses, the Tydings Committee ended up labeling McCarthy's accusations a "fraud" and a "hoax," and that the purpose of McCarthy's charges was to "confuse and divide the American people . . . to a degree far beyond the hopes of the Communists themselves."[11]

As might be expected, the liberal news media went berserk. Senator McCarthy was vilified and utterly discredited. In fact, his name became a word the *American Heritage Dictionary* defines as, "The practice of publicizing accusations of political disloyalty or subversion with insufficient regard to evidence." McCarthy died at age 48, a broken man.

However, in 1995 it was revealed that a top secret American intelligence operation known as the Venona project had decrypted a number of messages sent by Soviet Union intelligence agencies over the period 1940 to1948. They revealed that McCarthy had been absolutely right. This was confirmed by Soviet records that became known after the collapse of the Soviet Union.[12]

History professor and author Arthur Herman (who was coordinator of the Smithsonian's Western Heritage Program) wrote a book entitled *Joseph McCarthy: Reexamining the Life and Legacy of America's Most Hated Senator*. Herman said that the accuracy of McCarthy's charges "was no longer a matter of debate"—they are "now accepted as fact."[13]

Significance Of The US State Department "Mindset"

In making their policy and operating decisions, the President, his cabinet and advisers depend greatly on information and assessments fed to them by the State Department. These reports are based on information gathered from countless sources, which are analyzed by an army of career professionals. They choose what data is relevant and how it will be treated. They will decide what gets passed "up the line" and what slant will be put on it. Needless to say, this can have a great, if not determining effect on the decisions and actions of the President.

It has to be realized that while the top leadership in the State Department will change from one administration to the next, these career professionals stay. They are permanent fixtures, below the level of political vulnerability. Only people of like mind and belief will be hired into important, influential positions by the Department. And as in any government organization, they are hard to dislodge. Once a strongly held liberal / Socialist / Marxist mindset has become firmly established in a career-level government function, it is extremely hard, if not impossible, to remove without firing almost everyone and starting again from scratch. (That has never come even close to happening in the State Department.)

CHAPTER 2

AMERICAN COMPLICITY
IN EXPANDING COMMUNISM

INTRODUCTION

When the US State Department became anti-Capitalist and pro-Marxist in ideology, America began to covertly support and promote the expansion of Communism around the world. They were convinced that a centrally controlled Socialist form of government was the only viable workable government for the future. As such, they supported international Communism in its struggle against American Capitalism and "imperialism." They were working from the "inside" to restructure America and the West. The goal of their belief system was the establishment of a unified global government. This would supposedly be for the ultimate good of America, and essential to end world conflict. (See Appendix I.) This gave them "patriotic" justification for their actions.

To cover this clandestine support of Communism, America had a two-faced foreign policy—an official policy of being *against* Communism and *for* freedom, and a covert operating policy that worked to opposite ends. While America's official policies would undergo changes from one administration to the next, this fundamental covert operating policy remained essentially unchanged (except for the Reagan years).

This two-faced policy was acknowledged by General Lewis Walt, USMC (a Marine combat veteran of World War II, the Korean and Vietnam Wars) in his 1979 book, *The Eleventh Hour*, (written after he retired to warn the American public about what was happening). He experienced first-hand the inconsistency between our officially stated goals and the policies under which the military had to operate:

To put it in plain language, there have existed at least since 1945, two American policies—one public and one unspoken. The public policy has expressed the traditional ideals we all believe in—the right of people to be free, self-defense, peace through strength, opposition to Communism. The unspoken policy has expressed the thinking of the advisers who have influenced every American president—selling out oppressed peoples, unilateral moves towards disarmament, and accommodation with Communism [1]

As a result of this accommodation, from the 1940s through the 1970s, country after country fell to Communism—not as a result of American helplessness, mistakes or incompetence, but because it was planned that way.

THE PATTERN OF COMMUNIST TAKEOVER

There was often a definite and repeatable pattern in the way countries fell to Communism during the Cold War era with American covert complicity.[2] The liberal media and the State Department cooperated in the process.

1. A target nation would be chosen. It was invariably pro-western, anti-Communist, usually Christian, and lived in freedom.
2. The media would begin a relentless attack on problems within the target nation. ("Human rights" was often made into the major issue. Something can always be dug up in this category in any nation.)
3. Communist agitators would then move in and sow strife and dissension among the students, peasants, and poorer classes. Well-equipped guerillas then moved in as "freedom fighters."
4. The American media would support the Communist cause while never naming it as such. They would paint a rosy picture of the cause and typically described its leader as a "great agrarian reformer" in pursuit of "social justice."
5. America would then push for a "peace" conference to end the hostilities.
6. A "coalition government" would be formed, typically composed of one third Marxists, one third neutralists and one third nationalists.
7. The Marxists would then take over, either by intimidation, brute force, or with the help of the "neutralists," who invariably turned out to be Marxists.
8. When the target nation was finally inside the Communist orbit, the media coverage would cease. The public never heard about the follow-on purges, terror and human suffering, or the devastation of the economy. The media would simply move on to the next target.

NATIONS THAT FELL TO COMMUNISM

Nations that fell to communism with American complicity during the Cold War period included North Korea, Cuba, Laos, Iran, Nicaragua, China, Hungary, Central Africa, Cambodia, Rhodesia. Some details will be given surrounding the fall of China and Cuba.

CHINA (1948)

The tragic loss of China to Communism was facilitated by the United States government, with help from the news media. The American propaganda machine demonized the anti-Communist Chinese Nationalist leader, Chiang Kai-shek, while Mao Tse-tung (the Communist leader), was promoted as a "great agrarian reformer." A groundswell of support arose in America for a "coalition" government in China and the stopping of aid to the Nationalist Chinese. [3] In a well-researched article, *Who Lost China?* [4] Author Ann W. Carroll states:

> *[General George C.] Marshall was sent by President Truman as his personal representative to China, arriving on December 20, 1945. His specific instructions from Secretary of State Byrnes were to insist on a coalition government as a condition for continued aid to the Nationalists. [5] Because the Truman Administration had made a firm decision not to provide US combat troops to Chiang, [6] and since Marshall was convinced that Chiang could not win without US troops, he therefore agreed with the decision to insist on a coalition government as the only alternative, [7] though Marshall later stated in his testimony in the 1951 Senate hearings on the fall of China that he never had any doubts that Mao's forces were Marxist Communists. [8] Marshall held frequent meetings with Chiang or his delegates and with Mao's representative, Chou En-lai, and arranged two separate cease-fires in the civil war, in January and June of 1946. When Chiang would not cooperate with Marshall's efforts to set up a coalition government, Marshall ordered an arms embargo, in effect from July 29, 1946 through May 26, 1947.*

Some in Congress questioned this embargo and sent an envoy, General Wedemeyer, to China to study the effects of the embargo on Nationalist China. Wedemeyer recommended American aid to keep China from "falling into the hands of the Communists." His suggestion was suppressed by Presidential order. When last-minute support to the anti-Communist forces was reluctantly authorized by President Truman, the State Department made sure it would come too late. In an interview with Human Events magazine, M. Stanton Evans relates that when aid to the Chinese Nationalists under Chiang was cut off, Congress voted to send them emergency aid, "but that, too, was stalled, until Republican Sen. Arthur Vandenberg protested, and Truman, getting nervous, finally said, "I guess we'd better go ahead" with the aid to Chiang. Acheson [Secretary of State] then told his people, 'It is desirable that shipments be delayed where it is possible to do so without formal action.' " [9]

The outcome was inevitable. China was taken over by the Communists. The Chinese people lost their lands and their families. Anyone who resisted the takeover was killed. Over twenty million were liquidated. In 1958, a report from the Internal Security Subcommittee of the Senate Judiciary Committee, stated there had been a Communist conspiracy, and that "high American officials" had been "duped" into giving Communists their greatest victory, handing America a devastating defeat.[10] Very few Americans read the report, or even cared.

CUBA (1962)[11]

In the mid-1950s, Communist cells led by Fidel Castro were established within Cuba. Student riots were incited against the anti-Communist Batista government, the usual way the Communists did things. Then the media buildup began:

1. American TV networks sent cameras into the Cuban mountains to romanticize Castro. Pictures were sent back portraying him as a "Robin Hood"—a rebel leading a fight for social justice. The media went out of their way to dispel the idea that Castro's movement had a Communist complexion, and portrayed the Batista government as evil and corrupt and needing to be replaced.

2. *The New York Times* reporter Herbert Mathews wrote that Castro *"was the most remarkable and romantic figure to arise out of Cuba's history since Jose Marte, the hero of Cuba's wars of independence."*

3. In 1959, Ed Sullivan showed his nationwide TV audience an interview he had with Castro in Cuba in which he expressed his great admiration for Castro because he was "in the real American tradition of George Washington." Sullivan told his TV audience that Castro was "a fine young man who would come up with a democracy down there that America should have." (He later, retracted his support.)

America was being warned by university students in Cuba that Castro was indeed a Communist, and his lieutenants were agents of international Communism. However, a widely read Catholic newspaper disclaimed these warnings as lies, as did a Protestant newspaper, calling Castro a "great agrarian reformer."

Castro's popularity continued to grow in the US, and members of Congress were calling for the US to withdraw all aid to the Batista government. Finally, a government embargo was ordered on the Cuban government, and it was doomed. On January 1, 1959, Batista's anti-Communist government fell and Castro took over. (Prior to his promotion by the US, Castro had not been a real threat to the Cuban government.)

The State Department had been warned that aiding Castro would bring about a great victory in advancing international Communism, supposedly a far-reaching strategic defeat for the United States government. And in fact, Communism then rapidly spread as Cuba became the source of armaments for the Communist revolution in other Latin America countries.

After Cuba fell to Communism, the American government was determined to keep it that way. Several times, freedom-loving Cuban exiles tried to oust Castro. They were foiled by the American government every time, as revealed in the following newspaper headlines. The Colorado Springs, CO, Gazette of July 3, 1972: ANTI-CASTRO PLOT SMASHED BY U.S.

And then, when freedom-loving Cuban exiles again attempted to retake their country, the Tampa Tribune of August 16, 1977, announced; U.S. OFFICIALS FOIL EXILE RAID ON CUBA

COMMUNIST EXPANSION CONTAINED UNDER REAGAN

Throughout the entire presidency of Ronald Reagan, *not one square inch of any country fell to Communism!* An amazing fact considering that between 1976 and 1980, the spread of Communism had been accelerating. Reagan had a conservative, Christian-based worldview, in sharp contrast to previous presidents and those who came after him, Democrat or Republican. He spoke plainly, calling the Soviet Union exactly what it was—evil![12] He had a vision for freedom and began funding genuine freedom fighters all over the world and stopped the forward motion of the Communist movement.

Grenada

In the early 1980s, Grenada's Marxist-oriented Prime Minister, Maurice Bishop, aligned himself with Moscow. Hundreds of East-Bloc military advisers and personnel moved onto the tiny Caribbean island that was fast becoming another forward base to promote Soviet interests right on America's doorstep. Bishop was then assassinated and replaced by the even more violently anti-Western, hardline Communist Bernard Coard. Amidst the growing violence, the lives of nearly one thousand American medical students in Grenada were endangered. An appeal was made for America to do something.

In October 1983, President Reagan sent in a small liberating invasion force and, after a brief period of fighting, overcame all resistance. They captured hundreds of Cuban military and construction personnel and seized caches of Soviet-supplied arms. The American medical students were all rescued and two months later all American forces left the island. Democratic elections were held a year later.

Reagan's bold doctrine of undermining the Communist agenda by supporting anti-Communist forces was a major victory for liberty, sending a powerful and encouraging message to those fighting Communist forces all over the world. *It was the first time a Communist country had been liberated*, which repudiated the Soviet claim that once a nation became Communist, it would forever remain so.[13]

The people of Grenada showed their enthusiastic appreciation when Reagan visited them after the war and 99 percent of the entire population came out to greet and cheer this freedom-loving president!

However, when George H. W. Bush became president after Ronald Reagan in 1989, the support and promotion of genuine liberty came to an end. He did not have the same worldview as his predecessor—he was just another globalist, calling for a "New World Order" in which the United Nations would take on the active role of global security and management.

As we said in the Preface, in order to understand the present, we have to understand the past from which it came. The underlying purpose, goal and strategies of Vladimir Putin's Russia are coming directly out of those of the former Soviet Union. Similarly, the underlying purpose and mindset of America's present administration is an extension of those of the Cold War period. To better understand what is happening today, we therefore need to look in some detail at both Soviet and American Cold War policies.

CHAPTER 3

SOVIET POLICY

THE BASIS OF SOVIET POLICY

1. The Ultimate Marxist/Communist Goal Is Unchangeable

The primary objectives and operating policies of Marxists-Communists are well known and do not change. They have always been perfectly frank and open about them. They can be found in countless writings, speeches and web sites—and in how they act. This openness has been, and still is, *essential* to the Communist movement. The objectives and policies of Communism are the basis of its appeal to oppressed and self-seeking peoples all over the world, who want to see "justice" executed on segments of society and nations they consider to be their oppressors. (*Communism can have great appeal to both real and imaginary victims.*)

While the Soviets talked a lot about wanting "peace," the West had trouble grasping the fact that to Communists peace means *the entire absence of any opposition or competition to Communism*. World domination has always been their openly avowed goal. It is what binds the Communist movement together and is absolutely essential to its ideology. Melvin Laird, Secretary of Defense from 1969 to 1973 in the Nixon administration, wrote the following when he was a US Congressman:

> *The hard fact is that Communism will always remain true to its core because it has no choice. If the basic tenets of Communism were altered or even modified, the whole Communist empire would collapse . . . Communism cannot change; and to believe in the possibility of change is a madness almost as far from the true ordering of reason as the ideology itself. Communism, while it exists, must remain what it is. It is caught up in the most vicious circle in human history.* [1]

2. Nuclear War Is Both Survivable And Winnable

After an intensive post World War II study, the Soviets came to the conclusion that nuclear war was both survivable and winnable. This assumption was the basis of their military policy and arms buildup. [2] They knew perfectly well that nuclear war would *not* "end mankind"—a myth persistently promoted in the West. [3]

Soviet nuclear war theory was developed under the guidance of Marshall V.D. Sokolovskiy in the 1950s. A classified military report was developed known as the Ironbark Papers, which outlined how they would fight and win a nuclear war. An unclassified version of the report was published in the 1960s. [4] According to former CIA analyst William F. Lee, it showed that the Soviet Union sought to win a future nuclear war by creating offensive and defensive nuclear forces that would limit damage to the Soviet Union and deliver a decisive blow against America. [5]

3. Communist Morality

Soviet objectives and policies were pursued by whatever means needed to achieve their ends, motivated by impassioned hatred and violence. Communist morals are tied solely to the advancement of Communism. Lenin said:

> *Morality is that which serves to destroy the old exploiting society and to unite all the toilers around the proletariat, which is creating a new Communist society. Communist morality is the morality which serves this struggle.* [6]

An official 1950 statement from Radio Moscow, said: *"At the root of Communist morality, said Lenin, lies the struggle for the consolidation and the completion of Communism. Therefore, from the point of view of Communist morality, only those acts are moral which contribute to the building up of a new Communist society."* [7]

Communist activity against their enemies is motivated by hatred and violence, which is the necessary driving force for them to perpetrate their acts of savage brutality and barbarism. Stalin wrote in 1946 "It is impossible to conquer an enemy without having learned to hate him with all the might of one's soul" [8]

There never has been, nor will there be, any constraints on the means to the Marxist-Communist end. There is no correlation between political statements, agreements, rhetoric, and the desired end. As Ronald Reagan once said of Soviet diplomacy, "Words are one thing, actions are another."

SOVIET OPERATING POLICY

The Soviets set out to achieve overwhelming offensive strategic and tactical forces, as well as the capacity to survive a strategic nuclear strike by utilizing both active and passive defense systems. The foundation of their policy was to win a nuclear war through military might and effective homeland defense.

1. Develop Strategic And Tactical Military Power (Offensive Capacity)

The development of military might was the first priority of Soviet spending. Communists believe that "power comes from the barrel of a gun" and they intended to have the biggest gun. Their overall military objectives were to:

1. Develop the capacity for a preemptive strategic strike against America
2. Develop the necessary conventional forces to win a tactical war anywhere in the world and maintain territorial control of conquered countries.

2. Develop An Effective Anti-Ballistic Missile System (Active Defense)

The Soviets began a series of anti-ballistic missile (ABM) tests in the early 1960s, which were successful. [9] (An ABM shoots down incoming nuclear-armed intercontinental ballistic missiles—ICBMs.) A massive radar-networked ABM system was developed and deployed to protect Moscow, military targets and industrial centers.

3. Provide Nuclear Military And Industrial Shelters (Passive Defense)

The Soviets put a high priority on the passive protection of their military command and control functions and their entire industrial population from nuclear blast and fallout. By 1977, the Soviets had done the following. [10]

1. Placed their military command and control functions in deep, underground, nuclear-hardened facilities hundreds of feet below the surface. (Communist China has done the same thing.)
2. Protected some 60 million urbanized workers in vast underground bunker systems, said to be better than 90 percent effective against nuclear attack. This was effectively 100 percent of their industrial work force.

In the early 1970s I hired an engineer from Russia. He was Jewish and had been allowed to immigrate to Israel with his wife, and then came to America. He confirmed the presence of these hardened shelters, where at certain times they would practice taking shelter for a period. His wife worked at a different factory and went to a different shelter, but they could communicate by phone.

4. Bring Third-World Nations Under Communist Rule

The Soviets worked to bring third-world nations under Communism by taking full advantage of their poverty and social unrest. They employed any or all of the following means to facilitate the following:

1. Subversive guerilla warfare through proxies.
2. Open aggressive warfare through proxies.
3. Create confusion, disorder and collapse from within by the infiltration of political agents and agitators.
4. Provide military and domestic foreign aid to "soften" them and buy influence that could be used to the detriment of the West and the advantage of the Soviets.
5. Psychological warfare, employing the use of propaganda and spectacular achievements (such as Sputnik and the space program) to give the impression of Soviet invincibility and might.

The Soviets also contrived to disrupt or gain control of countries providing essential raw materials to the West (such as South Africa, a source of essential minerals).

5. Steal America's Secrets, Weaken Its Culture From Within

Soviet agents and sympathizers "invaded" the open societies of America and the West to learn their policy secrets, and steal their industrial and military know-how.

They also worked to "soften" America from within to expedite their downfall and takeover. American Marxists, their sympathizers and dupes were (and still are) used to undermine America's culture and strength by achieving the following:

1. Destroy the moral fiber, backbone of the American people.
2. Destroy the will of Americans to defend and fight for their "decadent" culture.
3. Destroy American national pride, patriotism and purpose.

This process came through the introduction of Marxist thinking and ideals into "higher academia" (the top universities and colleges) from where it spread throughout the public education system, and into the political process, the judicial system, the news and entertainment media, and to all the basic institutions of society (as discussed in an earlier section). *Once started, all that is required for the process to take over is for good men and women to be lulled into a self-consuming stupor and do nothing.* They will stand ignorantly and idly by, as the real "movers and shakers" of society set out to:

1. Trash Christian morality; promote the sexual revolution and remove all moral restraints (calling it "freedom"); promote homosexuality, incest, child-molesting, and all forms of sexual perversion; promote abortion; promote the drug culture and keep the American market well supplied.
2. Break down the traditional family by every possible means.

3. Rewrite/distort/discredit America's Christian heritage.
4. Revile patriotism and everything traditionally "American," concentrate on our faults and distort them out of proportion (while totally ignoring the faults of other nations) so that Americans will cease to love and care for their country.
5. Remove all Christian symbols and references from the public square, and infiltrate Christian institutions and subvert their beliefs.

This process boils down to the wholesale destruction of American culture and society by Marxists and mindless liberals *from within*. It has been called "cultural Marxism." It is discussed further in Chapter 10, America's Cultural Revolution.

6. Lull America And The West Into A False Sense Of Security

Offer America and the West the alluring promise of "peaceful" coexistence, which will lead to a false sense of security and a reduction of their military preparedness and resolve. The process effectively started with the internal dethronement of Stalin's image and an outward Soviet change toward the West over the last years of the Cold War through policies of:

Detente: The relaxation of strained relations or tensions (as between nations); also a policy promoting this.

Glasnost: Soviet policy permitting open discussion of political and social issues and freer dissemination of news and information.

Perestroika: Policy of economic and government reforms instituted by Soviet Secretary General Mikhail Gorbachev in the mid-1980s. (Merriam Webster Dict.)

When America's guard was sufficiently relaxed, the Soviets believed we would be ripe for the final blow that would destroy us. This has been part of their strategy since 1931, when the Lenin School on Political Warfare in Moscow taught that,

War to the hilt between Communism and Capitalism is inevitable ... Today, of course, we are not strong enough to attack ... To win we shall need the element of surprise. The bourgeoisie will have to be put to sleep. So we shall begin by launching the most spectacular peace movement on record. There will be electrifying overtures and unheard of concessions. The Capitalist countries, stupid and decadent, will rejoice to cooperate in their own destruction. They will jump at another chance to be friends. And as soon as their guard is down, we will smash them with our clenched fist. [11]

CHAPTER 4

THE CHANGED BASIS OF AMERICAN POLICY

Prior to the 1960s (particularly through World War II and the 1950s), the dominant principle behind America's defense policy was the belief that *peace could only be maintained through military strength.* The firm resolve to use it in the defense of liberty would discourage would-be tyrants of the world. In other words:

The PENALTIES of aggression will outweigh the gains of aggression

A COVERT, FOUNDATIONAL CHANGE

The Soviet Union launched the world's first satellite in 1957 (Sputnik-1). This was a spectacular achievement and a tremendous shock to the Western world—especially America's leaders and policy makers.

I was a college student in my home town of Melbourne, Australia at the time. Sputnik flew directly over the city on an evening I was taking a night class. We all went outside and watched it glide past overhead. It was traveling in a low elliptical orbit, and although it was only 23 inches in diameter, it could be seen very clearly. It was an unforgettable sight—*the beginning of the space-age!* Richard Pipes describes the frightening implication of Russia's achievement:

[The] situation changed dramatically in 1957 when the Soviets launched the Sputnik. This event, which their propaganda hailed as a great contribution to the advancement of science . . . represented in fact a significant military demonstration, namely, the [potential] ability of the Russians to deliver nuclear warheads against the United States homeland, until then immune from direct enemy threats.[1]

American strategists came to another, just as frightening conclusion. The Soviets had "leap-frogged" American rocket technology, and it was assumed they were rapidly catching up and about to surpass us in other areas also.

Recall that America's Marxist-minded policy analysts did not believe in the free enterprise system. They did not understand or appreciate the power and efficiency of free people operating in a free market economy. To them, a centrally-planned and controlled society was a superior way to marshal all the resources of a nation preparing for war. They believed such a system would unquestionably outperform an open, free-market society, and that in an all-out arms race, America was doomed.

A top-secret study completed in 1957on the arms race, known as the Gaither Report, painted a bleak picture of America's future security in light of the Soviet military buildup. This report (which was later declassified) convinced leading strategists and analysts that in the long run, the US could not hope to compete with the emerging military might of the Soviet totalitarian system.

As a result, the following rationale was presented to leading US military strategists in 1960 by Paul Nitze, who was later Deputy Secretary of Defense under Robert MacNamara in the Kennedy administration.

1. In the long run, we could not maintain our number-one military position.
2. It would then be extremely dangerous for America to be a strong number-two, since we would still be a grave military threat to the number-one Soviet Union.
3. The safest position for America—and the most stabilizing for world peace—was to be a much weaker number-two, so we would not be seen as a major strategic threat to the Soviets.

The idea of "safety-in-weakness" then became the unannounced basis of America's Soviet policy. This drastically altered the principle by which we hoped to ensure peace, which could be summarized and compared to our former policy as follows:

The REWARDS OF CONSTRAINT will outweigh the gains of aggression.

Securing peace then became more important than defending liberty. As a result, America's policy goals became:

1. Appease the Soviets in every way we could, and;
2. Greatly reduce our strategic military power so we would not be such a major threat to the Soviets, giving them no reason to launch a preemptive strike against America.

This change in policy would have been overwhelmingly rejected by the American people, so it was never formally announced. For most people, the idea of *safety in weakness* was simply *unbelievable*, so they did not have to be too concerned that a "whistle-blower" would be taken seriously. Some did tell about it, but they were basically ignored. One was Lt. General Daniel O. Graham, former director of the Defense Intelligence Agency and Deputy Director of the CIA, who wrote the following after retirement:

> *During Robert McNamara's tenure as Secretary of Defense, a curious rationale was conceived . . . for letting the Russians catch up. It went like this: the biggest danger of nuclear attack arises from Soviet strategic inferiority. Since they don't have a capability to ride out a US first strike, they stay nervous and might just attack us first. If we let them catch up, they will relax into our Mutual Assured Destruction strategy and forget about first strikes. This incredible notion not only froze US strategic systems at their mid-sixties levels, but formed much of the basis for opposition to fielding the Safeguard anti-ballistic missile system on the grounds it would "upset the strategic balance" in our favor![2]*

Another who spoke of it was Professor Richard E. Pipes, director of the Russian Research Center at Harvard (1968—1973), who said in a *Commentary* magazine that according to current American political thinking:

> *An American monopoly on nuclear weapons would be inherently destabilizing, both because it could encourage the United States to launch a nuclear attack, and, at the same time, by making the Russians feel insecure, causing them to act aggressively . . . In other words, to feel secure the United States actually required the Soviet Union to have the capacity to destroy it.[3]*

The execution of America's Cold War policy became a very delicate balancing act between outward firmness in the defense of freedom (for the sake of public appearance) and appeasing the Soviets, taking every precaution possible against antagonizing them. America's military threat to the Soviets had to be drastically reduced, while maintaining the appearance of superior military strength. How this was done is explained in the next chapter.

BASIC OVERT ASSUMPTIONS

The following four assumptions were an integral part of America's policy of Soviet appeasement and accommodation. They were openly acknowledged and established an environment in which the ultimate "necessity" of subjugating our sovereignty for the sake of world peace would be accepted by the public. They were the closest the administration came to exposing the real nature and purpose of its policies.

1. Nuclear War Is Unwinnable, Unsurvivable, Unthinkable

Despite all credible analysis to the contrary, many people in government believed—or said they believed—that full-scale nuclear war would end the human race. It was said that no one could survive a nuclear holocaust—there would be no winners. Everyone would lose. This belief was promoted with stubborn, emotional fervency. Fear is a powerful motivator, very effective in manipulating people to accept policies and actions they would otherwise reject. General Lewis Walt in his book contrasted the difference between the American and the Soviet attitude to nuclear war:

> At the end of World War II, major studies were conducted of strategic bombing. Our civilian strategists were so overwhelmed and shocked by the power of the atomic bomb that they made a fundamental decision that the invention of nuclear weapons had rendered war inoperable as a policy option. To them, nuclear war was unthinkable and unwinnable . . . Not surprisingly, Soviet thinkers drew a conclusion exactly the opposite of our Wall Street and Ivy League civilians. Soviet thinkers saw the nuclear weapon for exactly what it is; just a more powerful bomb; a more effective instrument of war. They came to the conclusion that nuclear war was not only thinkable but feasible and definitely winnable. [4]

2. Prevention Of Nuclear War Over-Rides Everything

This is the natural corollary of the first point. Presumably, the very existence of mankind is at stake! It then becomes easy (if not necessary) to accept the "reality" that government must prevent a nuclear war at any price. The fact that liberty would be the "price" was never mentioned. The public simply did not make the connection. Fear can paralyze, which distorts or negates the thinking process. No one seemed to question the false presuppositions upon which all this was based.

While this profound shift in values was never publically announced, we started to hear, over and over, "we must have peace at any price." The phrase "better red than dead" was sometimes heard in support of this.

3. Communism Is Changeable—Soviet Leaders Are Trustworthy

American leaders promoted the idea that Communism would "soften" and change. Arthur Schlesinger Jr., who later became Special Assistant to both Presidents Kennedy and Johnson, said in a 1947 article:

*Given sufficient time, the Soviet internal tempo will slow down. The ruling class will become less risk-minded, more security-minded. Greater vested interests will develop in the existing order. Russia itself will begin to fear the revolutionary tendencies which modern war trails in its wake . . . At the same time, US backing to the parties of the non-Communist left [such as socialist parties, not liberty-loving conservative parties] and US support for **vast programs of economic reconstruction** may go far toward removing the conditions of want, hunger and economic security, which are constant invitations to Soviet expansion . . . Can the United States conceive and initiate so subtle a policy? **Though the secret has been kept pretty much from the readers of the liberal press, the State Department has been proceeding for some time somewhat along these lines.** [5]*
(Emphasis added)

It is interesting to note that in this article, Schlesinger approvingly reveals that the US government, was (in 1947) already supporting socialist solutions, and had been so for "some time." He speaks of US "vast programs of reconstruction" (i.e. massive socialization, or government take-over) in the belief that they will go far toward alleviating hunger and want (which is pure, socialist philosophy).

Dean Rusk, Secretary of State for the Kennedy administration, very succinctly described the "Soviets-are-changeable" policy in a 1964 speech in which he said,

It is our policy to do what we can to encourage evolution in the Communist world toward national independence and open societies . . . to promote trends within the Communist world which lead away from imperialism, away from dictatorships, and toward independence and open societies with freely chosen governments, with which we can live in enduring friendship. [6]

The expectation that the Communists would mellow and change "toward open societies with freely chosen governments" is inconceivable in light of the brutal Soviet record of almost 50 years of blood-stained, totalitarian control. It was a blatant sales pitch to make the gullible American public feel good about being "nice" to the Soviet leaders and one day living in "enduring friendship" with them. The same message was also expressed by Under Secretary of State George Ball in testimony before the Senate Armed Services Committee in which he said,

I think one cannot rule out . . . that changes may take place in the individual nation states which make up the Communist bloc, which will transform

them from being dangerous, to the adoption of postures which will make them easier to live with in the world. [7]

The same unbelievable propaganda. And according to another senior administration official, Walt Whitman Rostow, Communist leaders would "mellow" and abandon their goals of world conquest and open the way for meaningful agreements "if we can [only] convince the Communists that we mean them no harm." [8]

The official party line of the American government was that the massive Soviet arms buildup was for defensive, not offensive, purposes. The buildup was represented as a natural reaction to their perceived threat from American military power. The Soviet-Communist leaders were repeatedly represented as wanting peace, and would be willing to live in peaceful coexistence with Western powers if they could only be made to understand our good intentions toward them. They were represented as decent, trustworthy fellows who simply had misconceptions about America's intent.

4. The United Nations Is The Great Hope For World Peace
When God is denied and replaced by the omnipotent State, there is only one hope for a "peaceful" world: a central authority responsible for the government and security of all peoples of the world. Wars are between nations, and it was deemed to be "obvious" that the elimination of independent nation-states would eliminate war. The necessity of a central world government was considered essential in light of the potential increase in proliferation of weapons of mass destruction.

This belief was held by America's leaders, policy makers and advisors during the Cold War era, with the exception of Ronald Reagan. The greatest obstruction to its fulfillment was a strong, independent, liberty-loving America. Most of them looked to the United Nations to fulfill the necessary function of world government, while the hardcore Marxists knew it would ultimately be a Communist government ushered in by the Soviet Union, not the UN.

In his State of the Union message on January 13, 1967, President Johnson made it obvious that he was a globalist thinker. He showed his contempt for nationalism (and therefore America as a sovereign nation) and his preference for "international partnership," (meaning the replacement of nationhood with international control and partnership with the Soviet Union) when he said:

As the first postwar generation gives way to the second, we are in the midst of a great transition from narrow nationalism to international partnership; from the harsh spirit of the Cold War to the hopeful spirit of common humanity on a troubled and threatened planet. . . We are shaping a new future of enlarged partnership in nuclear affairs, in economic and technological cooperation, in political consultation, and working together with the governments and people of Eastern Europe and the Soviet Union. [9]

The thinking of many of our politicians and leaders over the past forty years was well represented by Strobe Talbott, Deputy Secretary of State in the Clinton administration, in a 1992 Time Magazine essay in which he said:

Within the next hundred years . . . nationhood as we know it will be obsolete; all states will recognize a single, global authority . . . perhaps national sovereignty wasn't such a great idea after all . . . it has taken the events in our own wondrous and terrible [20th] century to clinch the case for world government. [10]

CHAPTER 5

AMERICA'S INCREDIBLE
POLICY IN OPERATION

As we have seen, America's new policy of "safety-in-weakness" required a drastic reduction in our military strength and the wholesale appeasement of Soviet aggression. This had to be accomplished while maintaining a public image of military strength and strong resolve in the defense of liberty. A seemingly impossible challenge, but the nation's leaders showed they were up to the task. Here is how it was accomplished.

SOVIET CONTAINMENT AND APPEASEMENT

1. Containing Soviet Aggression

America's "official" policy was to *contain* Soviet military aggression, while waiting patiently for the "inevitable" softening, or "mellowing," of their leaders and the relinquishment of their objective to conquer the world. There was never the slightest hint that we actually wanted to *defeat* the Soviets in any way. The policy of *inoffensive containment* was effectively adopted during the Truman administration and remained through the Carter administration. It was first suggested by career Foreign Service officer, George F. Kennan, in a 1947 *Foreign Affairs* article in which he wrote, "The main element of any United States policy toward the Soviet Union must be that of a long-term, patient but firm and vigilant containment of Russian expansive tendencies." [1]

"Containing" the Soviets translated into motivating them to be good by appeasing them—being outwardly firm but never advocating outright anti-Communism, or anything that could be construed as being anti-Soviet, like trying to "roll back" their power and liberate Eastern Europe. (Heaven forbid!)

2. Appeasing The Soviets

An essential part of appeasing the Soviets was to demonstrate trust and goodwill by putting ourselves in a position of being totally vulnerable to them, and supporting them economically and politically to the extent that the need to maintain a public image of "strength" allowed. President Kennedy's Assistant Secretary of Defense, Paul Nitze, illustrated the appeasement mentality of the Kennedy administration when, in an essay published just prior to his appointment, he equated survival with letting the Soviets have their own way; "If we cannot get them to agree to our viewpoint, we must accept theirs if we are to survive."[2] In other words—whatever we do, we mustn't push our argument or make a scene—we might aggravate them!

As the Kennedy administration made appeasement after appeasement, senators in both political parties began to challenge the "no-win" foreign policy. Most newspapers ignored the challenge, or ridiculed those who spoke out. However, the issue was finally addressed by a senior administration official, Walt Whitman Rostow, in a May 3, 1962 speech in Minneapolis,

> *It is sometimes asked if our policy is a no-win policy. Our answer is this—we do not expect this planet to be forever split between a Communist bloc and a free world. We expect this planet to organize itself in time on **principles of voluntary cooperation among independent nation states dedicated to human freedom. It will not be a victory of the United States over Russia.***[3] *(Emphasis added)*

The answer was, of course, an unqualified "yes" to the charge of having a no-win policy. He justified it by saying we can one day expect the Soviet Union to join us (and other independent nations such as western Europe, Canada, Australia) to become "dedicated to human freedom." (One big happy family!) We therefore have no cause to worry about war between us. A very reassuring message for gullible Americans to help them to accept our appeasement policy. This is just what we would want the Soviets to hear. In accomplishing its purposes, the statement was masterful!

Then President Jimmy Carter's Secretary of State, Cyrus Vance, in an interview with *Time* Magazine in 1978, said; "Negotiating with the Soviet Union is sometimes a frustrating experience, but at the end of the road, when you reach an agreement, they stick to their bargains."[4] ("Stick to their bargains"? Incredible! Based on what? Certainly not on history!) This follows right along with Rostow's above statement to give gullible Americans "assurance" that in the long run, we have nothing to worry about—we can trust them.

Think about what these men were saying. The history of Soviet atrocities and treaty violations was no secret—available to anyone who can read. The administration certainly knew the true nature of the people they were dealing with. They knew the Soviets had broken every treaty they had ever signed (with the exception of the treaty Stalin had made with another tyrant, Hitler, who broke it first!). They have lied, cheated, manipulated, and deceived at every possible turn. To present them as a reasonable, trustworthy bunch to whom we should be nice and accommodating should have been taken as an insult to the intelligence of those to whom such statements were directed. (Perhaps the task of pulling the wool over our eyes was not so challenging after all!)

UNILATERAL DISARMAMENT

As a general policy, the disarmament of America was openly declared to be a necessary requirement for "world peace." Keep in mind the Marxist definition of "world peace" is the world-wide absence of opposition to Marxism. The implicit argument was that by eliminating weapons of war, we would eliminate war itself. (The same assumption is behind the belief that by legally eliminating private gun ownership, we will eliminate gun-crimes.) It was implied to be the "responsible" thing to do. So America, as a responsible nation, should take the first step. Never mind the Russians. When they see our responsible attitude, they will follow right along.

This was, of course, part of implementing America's safety-in-weakness policy without naming it as such. The policy was more for Soviet than American consumption, letting them know that we had no intention of being a military threat to them. We had to be seen as a peace-loving people who not only *would* never attack them, we were willing to put ourselves in a position that we *could* never attack them. The best way to show this was to openly show our willingness to *unilaterally* totally disarm.

As a first step to this end, President Kennedy proposed a "general and complete disarmament" under United Nations control in a speech made at the opening of the United Nations on September 25, 1961. ***An astonishing plan for the specific disarmament of the United States was outlined in the 1961 Department of State Publication 7277—"Freedom from War: The United States Program for General and Complete Disarmament in a Peaceful World."*** [5]

According to this official State Department publication, the United States would abolish its Army, Navy, Air Force, and all its nuclear weapons in three stages, after which America would be totally subject to a United Nations Peace Force. The production of nuclear weapons and their delivery systems in the US would be banned, and all our existing nuclear warheads would be transferred to UN control. If the reader has trouble believing this, the whole State Department publication can be read on line at the web site given in the above reference. The document specifically called for the elimination of all weapons and armaments *except* those necessary to maintain "internal order," making us a police state. It stated:

> *The disbanding of all national armed forces and the prohibition of their reestablishment in any form whatsoever other than those required to preserve internal order and for current contributions to United Nations peace force; The elimination from national arsenals of all armaments, including all weapons of mass destruction and the means for their delivery, other than those required for a United Nation's peace force and for maintaining internal order.* [6]

Senator John Tower (R-TX) labeled the document "one of the most incredible proposals ever to emerge from the State Department." He said:

> *As skeptical as I have always been of the measure of good sense and loyalty within the State Department, I would never have believed that these people that we call our diplomats, could so completely and unabashedly advocate the surrender of American rights and sovereignty until this bulletin appeared. . . If more of the American people knew about this scheme there would be a nationwide uproar that would make the reaction to the Alger Hiss scandal look like another era of good feeling by comparison* [7]

In response to Senator Tower's statement, Senator Joseph Clark (D-PA.) supported and "clarified" the State Department's proposal for the complete disarmament of the United States as the "fixed, determined, and approved policy of the government of the United States, as laid down by President Kennedy." He further said that it was "the kind of program which Congress envisioned when, last summer, it passed the statute creating the Arms Control and Disarmament Agency."[8]

The Arms Control and Disarmament Agency was created when Congress passed Public Law 87-297. It was charged with managing disarmament negotiations, conducting technical research in the disarmament field, and instituting a public relations campaign to "condition" the American people to accept disarmament. [9]

On April 18, 1962, the Kennedy administration announced further plans for unilateral disarmament in three stages, prior to subjecting our country to a permanent UN peace force. In a June 10, 1963 speech, President Kennedy publicly confirmed this when he said; "Our primary long-range interest in Geneva . . . is **general and complete disarmament**, designed to take place by stages." [10] (Emphasis added.)

America's announced plan for complete, unilateral disarmament was totally impractical to implement. *And they knew it!* Political maneuvering is one thing, but if the public saw it was becoming a reality, there would be rioting in the streets. *Not even mindless Americans would stand for that!* The whole plan appears to have been staged to impress the Soviets of our willingness to be totally vulnerable. After Kennedy left the scene the whole ridiculous charade was quietly dropped from public view.

COVERT REDUCTION OF STRATEGIC STRENGTH

However, actual reductions in our military strength had to be implemented to make our "peace through weakness" policy a reality. They would have to be very significant to allow the Soviets to surpass us—without alarming the public as to what was happening. To achieve this, the following actions were taken.

1. Operational Strategic Weapons Scrapped

President Kennedy's Defense Secretary, Robert MacNamara, destroyed more US strategic weapons by simply declaring them obsolete than could have been destroyed by a full-blown Soviet surprise attack. These weapons were still highly effective, with many years of operational life left when they were scrapped.

Strategic nuclear-armed bombers were the mainstay of America's nuclear delivery system. In 1960 we had 2,710, but over his tenure as Secretary of Defense, McNamara scrapped all but 665—an incredible 75 percent reduction. [11]

1. The entire force of 1,400 B-47 strategic bombers were scrapped. They were declared "obsolete," but Air Force General Thomas Power said they would have been an effective force through the end of the twentieth century. [12]

2. The number of B-52 strategic bombers (then the world's most advanced bomber) was first reduced from 630 to 585, then McNamara announced plans to scrap all but 240. [13]

3. All 129 Atlas ICBM's were scrapped. They carried warheads six to eight times more powerful than the Minuteman ICBMs that replaced it. [14]

4. All of our Titan I strategic missiles were scrapped, even though they carried seven times the payload of the Minuteman missile. Before

he left office, McNamara announced plans for scrapping all Titan II missiles as well. [15]

5. All US intermediate and medium-range strategic missiles deployed in Europe were scrapped, in spite of the fact that the Soviets had 750 similar missiles threatening NATO cities and bases in Europe. All of the Thor and Jupiter missiles installed in Turkey, Italy, and England were also scrapped. [16]

2. Strategic Bases And Operations Closed Down

Many strategic operations and bases vital to America's defense were shut down.

1. The entire force of 600 carrier-based strategic nuclear-armed bombers were withdrawn from carrier service, and the fifteen aircraft carriers from which they operated were taken off strategic alert in 1965. *These bombers had been our most reliable deterrent against a surprise Soviet nuclear attack on the United States, since aircraft carriers at sea could not be targeted by Soviet missiles.* [17]

2. The Strategic Air Command (SAC) was closed down. This had been a continuous airborne alert by which the US always had nuclear-armed bombers in the air, invulnerable to a Soviet first strike and ready to instantly counter-strike—a huge deterrent to a surprise Soviet attack.[18]

3. Strategic bomber bases in Morocco, France, England, and Spain were closed and their bombers returned to America. [19] Forty-five missile-launching bases in Turkey and Italy were declared "obsolete" and closed. [20]

3. Strategic Weapon Programs Cancelled, Billions Wasted

Many highly effective weapon systems were developed, proven effective in prototype testing, and then canceled. This had a double advantage for our political leaders. It kept us from putting the most advanced weapons into operation that would have guaranteed our strategic superiority, and the billions wasted on them would keep the defense budget high to maintain the public facade that we had a strong military that was "defending freedom." Some of the many examples are:

1. The B-70 Bomber and the Skybolt Missile, a Mach 3, high-altitude strategic delivery system (proven successful in the prototype phase), was *canceled* after spending *$9 billion*. Defense Secretary McNamara justified this by saying existing bombers carrying the Skybolt air-to-ground missile could do the job just as effectively at much lower cost. However, shortly after this, all production of long-range bombers

was stopped. Then the Skybolt missile was *cancelled* after spending *$2 billion,* despite the strong objections of all competent military authority. [21]

2. The Pluto Missile, a research, atomic propelled, low-flying, high-speed missile with around-the-world range, described as the "most powerful missile yet conceived," was *scrapped* after spending *$600 million* on initial research. [22]

3. The Navaho Cruise Missile was *scrapped* after spending *$4 billion* and the Dyna-Soar Orbital Bomber was *scrapped* after spending *$400 million* on development. [23]

4. The Truck Mounted Mobile Medium Range Ballistic Missile was *scrapped* after spending *$100 million* on development. [24] Being truck-mounted meant it was mobile, and therefore invulnerable to a Soviet ICBM surprise attack.

5. The Nike-Zeus Anti-Ballistic Missile system was shelved and later canceled. [25] This, *despite the fact* that on April 17, 1963, the Defense Department acknowledged that the Soviets had an anti-missile system deployed around Leningrad with the capacity to intercept and destroy incoming American Polaris missiles. [26]

4. Strategic Weapon Firepower Drastically Reduced

Between the mid-60s and 70s, the US spent some *$4 billion* on defense *without adding one single strategic nuclear weapon* to our arsenal, while the Soviets added over 2,000 ICBMs and SLBMs (submarine-launched ballistic missiles) to theirs!

Between the early 1960s and the mid-1970s, the total firepower of all US stockpiled nuclear weapons (in megatons, or equivalent million tons of conventional explosives) was reduced by about 60 percent. Over the same period, it is estimated that the Soviet nuclear stockpile increased as much as 20 times. [27] And in 1975 their actual *deployed* firepower was over seven times that of the US (see Appendix III).

Total US firepower and its effectiveness was significantly reduced when the single warhead in many missiles was replaced with multiple warheads which could be independently targeted. Such missiles were called Multiple Independent Re-entry Vehicles (MIRVs). However, each warhead had to be very small in order to accomplish this, and the total firepower of the missile was *greatly* reduced.

While a small warhead of the size that was dropped on Hiroshima and Nagasaki (0.015 and 0.022 megatons respectively) will have a devastating effect on "soft" civilian targets, it would be ineffective against a well "hardened" target. On the assumption that most US missiles were intended for hardened Soviet military targets, "MIRVing" them very significantly reduced their chance of military target destruction. While the Soviets "MIRVed" some of their missiles, the firepower of their smallest warhead was 0.5 megatons, over 12 times more powerful than our smallest "MIRVed" warhead (See Appendix III).

VULNERABILITY TO NUCLEAR DESTRUCTION

1. The "Mutual Assured Destruction" Policy (Mad)

The US intentionally made itself unilaterally defenseless against a Soviet attack upon its civilian population. This was achieved by deceiving the American public into believing that the Soviet population would be just as vulnerable, so we could be assured that neither side would attack the other. This deadly deception was called "Mutual Assured Destruction," with the appropriate acronym, MAD.

This policy was developed by Defense Secretary Robert McNamara, and called for the US and the Soviet Union to provide *no active or passive defense* for their civilian populations. The population of each nation would, in effect, be held hostage by the other nation. The idea of incinerating millions of unprotected innocent civilians was considered (by America's strategists) to be so awful that it was utterly unthinkable. Soviets strategists however, did not share this view. The awfulness of this total vulnerability was promoted to the American public as being the most powerful deterrent imaginable to nuclear war. Supposedly, MAD would "assure" our safety!

For this policy to work and ensure a "stable nuclear deterrence," the population of each nation had to be defenseless against a nuclear attack on its population, with their strategic forces able to sufficiently survive a surprise nuclear strike so it could counter-strike the other side and incinerate *its* population. Assured *mutual* destruction. This meant that each side could not try to shelter its people from nuclear attack, and their ABM (Anti-Ballistic Missile) defense had to be limited in scope so it could not prevent population destruction.

However, there was absolutely nothing mutual about it. The Soviets never agreed to it—formally or informally! America's leaders obviously knew that, but most certainly did not want the American public to know it. However, this was recognized in an "official" setting just recently. In May, 1999, the effectiveness of the Cold War ABM Treaty was historically analyzed at a United States Senate Committee on Foreign Relations hearing on *US Strategic and Arms Control Objectives*. Testimony was given by Dr. Keith B. Payne, president of the National Institute for Public Policy Faculty, Georgetown University School of Foreign Service, in which he stated "Former senior Soviet officials, however, have since explained repeatedly, and at length, that the ABM Treaty did not reflect Soviet acceptance of US notions of deterrence and mutual vulnerability." [28]

The lack of any Soviet agreement was of no concern to America's Cold War leaders. They fully implemented MAD as the mainstay of our supposed nuclear deterrence policy. We deactivated our designated shelters by simply removing all the "Fall-out Shelter" signs. We also dismantled the single, limited ABM system which we had just developed and built. On the other hand, the Soviet Union built hardened shelters for their entire industrial work-force and developed a massive ABM system to shoot down incoming ICBMs. (Covered in the next section.)

General Walt pointed out what was happening in his book. "This stripping of our defense forces has been a deliberate policy move on the part of our civilian defense officials. They believe that by baring our population to the Soviet sword, we demonstrated our peaceful intentions. The error in their thinking was to believe that the Soviet Union would follow our example. The Soviets have reacted in an ominously opposite manner. While we cut back, they've built, until today they have the world's most extensive air defense and civil defense systems." [29]

MAD never was a "mutual" program. It rendered our civilian population vulnerable to destruction, while the Soviets actively defended theirs. *By intent, it assured that only America's population could be destroyed.* Thus, we demonstrated our "good will" toward the Soviets. ("See, we mean you no harm. We trust you with our very lives. You have absolutely no reason to fear us or to hurt us!")

2. The Anti-Ballistic Missile (Abm) Treaty

The original ABM treaty of 1972 between the Soviet Union and America provided that both nations dismantle the missile defense systems they had each started, and promised to build no more.

This treaty was an absolutely essential part of America's MAD policy, as it supposedly ensured—by signed agreement—that our cities would be totally vulnerable to nuclear attack. In fact, National Security Advisor Henry Kissinger (later Secretary of State) testified before a Senate hearing in 1972 that *the ABM Treaty would ensure that foreign missiles had a "free ride" to any target within the US.* [30]

The treaty was amended in 1974 to allow the deployment of 100 interceptor ABM's by each side at a single site. The US placed its "allowed" ABM site in North Dakota to defend its nuclear retaliatory forces, rather than the nation's capital. However, the site was *deactivated and dismantled* after less than 6 months of operation!

The Soviet Union totally ignored the ABM treaty and actively pursued both active and passive defense measures and built an ABM system far beyond the terms of the treaty. America not only abided by the treaty, we went *beyond* compliance by refusing to take advantage of the limited ABM system that the treaty allowed. *And this despite the blatant, obvious Soviet violations,* which should have removed any *legal* or *moral* obligation we had to maintain compliance. In fact, our government had a *moral obligation* to discard the treaty and *protect its citizens from the menace posed by the Soviet violations!*

Our dogged adherence to treaties and agreements in the face of violations was just another signal to the Soviets of our good will and our *total and complete trust in them!*

3. The Strategic Arms Limitation Treaties (Salt I, Salt II)

The SALT I and II treaties were preceded by several years of talks and negotiations. Their overall purpose was agreement between the two superpowers on "freezing the number and characteristics of their strategic nuclear offensive and defensive vehicles."

According to the terms of these treaties, a limitation was placed on *the number of strategic missile launchers* (not missiles). This was very significant, as it eventually put America at a huge disadvantage. We could only fire one missile at a time from each ICBM silo launcher, because it could took weeks after a launch to repair the silo walls from the effects of the rocket blast. On the other hand, the Soviets could fire multiple successive ICBMs from their silos because of their "cold-launch" rapid re-fire ability. It was estimated they could have up to five missiles that could be rapidly fired from each silo.

The cold-launch technique ejected the missile from its silo with compressed air before the rocket engines were ignited. This saved the concrete walls of the silo from being wrecked by the rocket blast. The idea was first proposed in America, but rejected. Obviously it would greatly increase our strike capability, *something they did not want to do.* The idea was described in detail in *Aviation Week and Space Technology* magazine.[31] It was picked up and executed by the Soviets.

As well as having this rapid re-fire advantage, the Soviets were also given a huge advantage in the actual number of launchers as well. By the terms of the treaty, the US was limited to 1,054 fixed ICBM silo launchers and 656 SLBM submarine-based launchers. The Soviets were allowed 1,398 ICBM launchers and 950 SLBM launchers, a respective 33 percent and 45 percent advantage over the US!

In order to justify the locked-in advantage given to the Soviets by the SALT I treaty, Secretary of State Henry Kissinger pointed out that the Soviets were building up their ICBMs and SLBMs at a very substantial annual rate, while the Americans were building none and had no plans to build any. (Amazingly, nobody asked him "why not?") Therefore, in "freezing" the strategic levels at that point, Kissinger claimed that America was really getting a great deal, because the treaty guaranteed that the missile gap in favor of the Soviets would get no bigger! Kissinger's own words are very revealing. "Any time over the next five years we were confronting a numerical margin that was growing, and *a margin, moreover, which we could do nothing to reverse in that five-year period.*[32] (Emphasis added)

To say that we could do nothing about it was absurd! It was in fact an outright lie! At that time we had ongoing programs for the production of new Minuteman III ICBMs and new Poseidon SLBMs. We had operational missile production lines capable of being ramped up to turn out over 2,000 ICBMs and SLBMs a year![33] America could have closed the gap and gone well beyond them over that five-year time period had we wanted to.

I worked for a company that made a sub-system for the Minuteman missile. Our production lines were ready—we would have welcomed new orders!] There is no question that America's industrial might and capacity for innovative technology was far greater than that of the Soviet Union. *There was absolutely nothing stopping us from closing the missile gap—except the will of our own leaders!* Obviously, they did not want to close a gap they had very purposefully generated! Phyllis Schlafly and Rear-Admiral Chester Ward, in their book about Kissinger, said, "Tragically for US national security, the Kissinger argument worked. It worked even against the more intelligent, dedicated, and knowledgeable critics of SALT. As Kissinger had foreseen, his assumption [*slated in the guise of a "fact"*] that the United States was helpless to close or even narrow the missile gap was not challenged."[34]

4. Soviet Violations Of The Salt And Abm Treaties

Many concerned former American leaders, such as Defense Secretary Melvin Laird, Admiral Zumwalt, and Paul Nitze, documented and published the many known Soviet violations to the SALT and ABM treaties. As stated earlier, the Soviets had no regard for these treaties, while the Americans adhered strictly to their letter. Furthermore, as previously noted, America stuck religiously to the terms of the ABM treaty even *after the demise of the Soviet Union*, when it was no longer a valid contract! When one party to a contract dies, the contract is no longer binding unless the terms of the contract itself require its perpetuity after the demise of one of the parties. The ABM Treaty had no such provision.

When the Soviets continued to ignore the terms of the treaties they signed, it was blatantly obvious that they were intent on achieving military superiority and had not the slightest intention of reducing their strategic forces.

The *Committee on the Present Danger*, a private group of former diplomats and men of former high political office, was created to inform the public on national defense issues. A report from them was published in 1977 in *US News and World Report* which said.

> From the beginning of SALT [Strategic Arms Limitations Talks] at Helsinki in 1969, the Soviet objective has been to preserve the USSR's gains and momentum, while encouraging maximum constraint upon US programs. In the classic Soviet fashion, negotiations have been regarded as a means of stalling and impeding the adversary's momentum while maintaining its own.[35]

5. America's Unannounced "Pause" Policy

In order to achieve what the unilateral disarmament intellectuals called "crisis stability" in the event of a surprise Soviet nuclear attack, America had a policy by which we would "pause" before making any counterstrike. This was so we could "negotiate." While this was never formally announced with regard to the strategic defense of the United States, it *was* our announced policy with regard to the tactical defense of NATO. In fact, it so enraged French president Charles de Gaulle that he pulled France out of NATO![36]

However, Defense Secretary Arthur Schlesinger made it clear that we *would* pause in the event of a Soviet surprise attack. In the Department of Defense (DOD) annual report for 1974, he described the essential features of our strategic posture, stating that we should have high confidence of being able to ride out a massive surprise attack and penetrate enemy defenses "with the ability to withhold an assured destruction reserve for an extended period of time." In order to restrain any unauthorized attempt by US forces to retaliate against such a surprise Soviet attack, the National Command Authorities would be required "to direct the employment of the strategic forces in a controlled, selective and restrained fashion." In addition, we should avoid "any combination of forces that could be taken as an effort to acquire the ability to execute a first-strike disarming attack against the USSR."[37] Schlafly and Ward comment:

> It would be difficult for a US Secretary of Defense to use any language better calculated to assure the Soviets that they can execute a massive disarming strike against the United States without triggering a retaliatory strike against Russia. Our defense chief is assuring the enemy that we have the ability to withhold for an extended period of time any and all retaliation—in other

words the "pause."... The need for a pause for such an "extended period" is to provide time for the surrender of the United States. [38]

INVALUABLE ASSISTANCE

1. American Counter-Intelligence Agencies Dismantled

During the 1970s, a whole series of decisions and actions destroyed the internal security of the United States. According to a Human Events article:

> *Civil-service authorities decided that membership in the Communist Party was not a barr to federal employment, even in sensitive positions. The FBI, which was supposed to do checks to see if such individuals were connected to revolutionary groups, acknowledged in 1979 that they were out of this business also.* [39]

Syndicated columnist, Ralph De Toledano, a longtime student of Communist activity in America and author of *Seeds of Treason*, revealed the state of America's internal security in 1987.

> *It will come as a shock to most Americans that the United States has no domestic intelligence or security agency. The FBI is barred from gathering information on a terrorist group or subversive apparatus until there is what lawyers call a "criminal nexus." In simple English, this means that the FBI cannot investigate or infiltrate a suspected terrorist organization until an act of violence has been committed.*

De Toledano went on to explain how this came about:

> *This situation has existed since 1976, when the late Democratic Senator Frank Church held hearings that pilloried the FBI, CIA and other security agencies. Their crime, in his eyes, was that they were attempting to ferret out terrorist activity before the bombs exploded. The Church Committee, assisted by the national media, put the kibosh on further information gathering by the FBI, which Mr. Church considered nefarious, ungentlemanly, and unconstitutional. This left the country without a domestic security agency to protect it.* [40]

Syndicated columnist W. Stanton Evans supplied some statistical evidence in a column titled, "How US Internal Security Was Destroyed." Evans reported, "The number of domestic security cases under FBI investigation dropped from 24,414 in 1973 to 51 in 1983." [41]

Evans explains that the situation became so bad, that according to official testimony, the FBI could not even maintain *a file* on a self-professed Communist organization, even if they openly advocated violence and published their intention of infiltrating the US military because no crime had yet been committed. The then FBI Director, William Webster, is quoted as saying, "we're practically out of the domestic security field." [42]

General Walt also warned the American public of the intelligence situation in his book, *The Eleventh Hour.*

> *The ability of both the FBI and the CIA to conduct counter-intelligence activities has been reduced to almost total incapacity. All of this has come at a time in our history when the Soviet Union has stepped up its subversive activities everywhere in the world. It is estimated that on any given day there are as many as 25,000 Communist bloc nationals in the United States— diplomats, journalists, trade representatives, academics, entertainers, sports figures, and merchant seaman. A great percentage of them are members of the Soviet KGB or are working on special assignment for the KGB . . .*

> *Communists have for years sought the destruction of the House Committee on Un-American Activities. Civil libertarians in Congress closed it down. Communists have long sought to weaken the FBI's and CIA's anti-Communist abilities; the liberal Congress and the executive branch have done the job for them.* [43]

In addition, many Supreme Court decisions in the 1950s and 1960s contributed greatly to crippling US internal security programs.

The result (and intended purpose) of dismantling our counterintelligence agencies was to covertly assist the Soviets in surpassing us militarily by making it easy for them to infiltrate our military and defense industry establishments and obtain our secrets. Putting out the obvious "welcome" mat for Soviet agents was a further demonstration of our willingness to be vulnerable and trust them.

2. Soviet Technology And Industry Buildup By The West

Soviet technology and their industrial and military complex has come, directly or indirectly, from the United States and its allies. [44] This massive transfer, which began under President Woodrow Wilson right after the Russian Bolshevik Revolution in 1917, has been accomplished through trade, direct grants, loans (many of which were later forgiven), and direct technical assistance. At the end of

World War II, Josef Stalin acknowledged the role America had played, as reported by US ambassador to the Soviet Union, Averell Harriman,

> *Stalin paid tribute to the assistance rendered by the United States to Soviet industry before and during the War. [Stalin] said that about two-thirds of all the large industrial enterprises in the Soviet Union has been built with the United States' help or technical assistance.* [45]

Stalin could have added that the other one third came from Germany, France, Britain, and Italy. This massive technical assistance continued throughout the Cold War era.

Following are just a few examples of this aid and assistance, giving the Soviet Union the industrial and technological capacity to build everything required for modern high-tech warfare.

1. The Soviet battle-tank industry came directly from the United States. A plant was set up at Stalingrad in the 1930s, capable of producing 50,000 Caterpillar-type tractors a year (an army tank is a caterpillar vehicle). The plant was first completely constructed in the United States, then dismantled and reconstructed in the Soviet Union by American engineers. Other "farm tractor" plants were later built at Kharkov and Chelyabinski using American machine tools and equipment. These plants later produced self-propelled guns, armored cars, and the Soviet T-37 battle tank. [46]

2. The Soviets bought fifty-five Rolls-Royce turbojet aircraft engines (the most advanced in the world at the time) from Great Britain in 1946. They were reproduced in quantity using American and German-supplied machine tools. These engines powered the MIG-15 fighters used in the Korean War. [47]

3. All Soviet iron and steel technology came from the US and its allies. They use open hearth electric furnaces, and wide strip mills—developed in America and shipped to the Soviet Union as "peaceful trade." In the 1970s, the Soviets had the largest iron and steel plant in the world, a copy of the US Steel plant in Gary, Indiana, built by the American McKee Corporation. Soviet tube and pipe making technology (essential for missiles, aircraft and warships) also came from the West. [48]

4. Soviet truck-building capacity came from the West. The Gorki truck plant in Russia was built in the 1930s by Ford and the Austin Company of England. It produced a whole line of military vehicles

used against Americans in Vietnam. *Then while this war was in progress*, Gorki received further equipment from the US to expand their facilities!

In 1968, FIAT of Italy built a plant in Volgograd in the Soviet Union that was larger than the Gorki plant, using American suppliers. Dean Rusk, US Secretary of State in the Kennedy and Johnson administrations, and Walt Rostow, Johnson's National Security Adviser, told Congress and the American public that the FIAT plant could *not* produce military vehicles and that this was purely "peaceful trade." This was totally untrue. Any vehicle manufacturing plant can be set up to produce military vehicles.

Then, during the Nixon administration, while the Vietnam War was in progress, *American and other Western technology built the largest heavy truck plant in the world by the Kama River, in the very heart of the Soviet Union. It produced trucks used to transport supplies and equipment down the Ho Chi Minh trail in Vietnam for the Vietcong to fight the American army. Furthermore, American taxpayers underwrote the financing of this massive plant through the Export/Import Bank, Chase Manhattan.* [49]

5. In the late 1960s, Soviet missiles were extremely inaccurate. According to Abraham Shifrin, a former Defense Ministry official, they could hardly find the United States, let alone a specific target within it. However, by the late 1970s, their accuracy was so improved that Soviet missiles were capable of hitting a target within the United States as small as the White House. This dramatic improvement in accuracy was partly made possible in 1972 when, under President Nixon and National Security Adviser Henry Kissinger, government approval was given to export to the Soviet Union specialized machine tools manufactured by the Bryant Chucking Company of Springfield, Vermont, capable of producing extremely high-precision miniature ball bearings, absolutely essential to the accuracy of a missile guidance system. [50]

6. In 1973, the Control Data Corporation was given government approval to provide technical assistance to the Soviet Union enabling them to set up a plant to manufacture computer chips (absolutely essential for modern warfare). [51]

When the administration was questioned about these policies, the standard line was, "this is peaceful trade—it's a way to build friendship between us." While it is true that peace leads to trade, it is *not* true that trade leads to peace. American trade with Germany and Japan increased greatly in the 1930s, helping them to prepare for war against us. These examples barely represent the tip of the iceberg of the massive buildup of Soviet technology and industry by the United States and other Western powers. We created the high-technology capacity of our own enemy. By the early 1970s, the United States was spending some $80 billion a year on defense against an enemy which we ourselves had equipped.

I personally experienced the betrayal of our government in giving specialized technology to the Soviet Union the early 1970s. The company I worked for was asked by the government to gather all the design information, specifications and formulae for a particular hi-tech product for which we were the major supplier in the West for both commercial and military aircraft. It would be passed on to the Soviet Union for "peaceful" application to commercial aircraft, even though the technology was obviously just as applicable to military aircraft. Since I had design engineering responsibility for the product line, I was told to gather the requested information. I strongly objected to aiding and abetting our enemy and refused to be involved. A higher level manager simply came in and got the requested information. I must add that my company had a lot of big government contracts at the time, and we may well have had little choice in the matter.

Over 110,000 American servicemen were killed in the Korean and Vietnam wars, largely by weapons utilizing American technology made with machine tools and equipment supplied by America and the West!

We need to look next at what really happened in the tragic Vietnam War.

CHAPTER 6

VIETNAM – WHAT REALLY HAPPENED

INTRODUCTION

America was involved in two wars against Communist aggression during the Cold War era—the Korean War and the Vietnam War. The casualties were shocking—over 54,000 American serviceman died in Korea and over 58,000 in Vietnam. The Vietnam War was by far the most politically and culturally significant of the two wars, and is the one we will concentrate on here. However, by way of introduction, we need to say a little about the Korean War that preceded it.

The Korean War was a no-win war by intent. We could have driven the Communists out of all of Korea, but we were not allowed to. This was the first time that something like this had happened in American history, and it paved the way for the Vietnam War (which was the same kind of war). It was also the first time that American troops were not under American control—they were under United Nations control. We learn of the nature of the war from General Walt, who commanded the Fifth Marine Regiment in Korea. In his book, he describes how the war was run:

> *At the time, I was politically naive. Like all American military professionals, it had been drummed into my head that politics was the province of civilians. My job was to fight—someone else would decide who and when and under what conditions. Little did I dream that the civilian leadership was willing to sacrifice American lives in no-win wars and to keep this policy secret from the American people.* [1]

> *It bothered me deeply that I was required to submit 24 hours in advance a detailed plan of attack for approval by UN Command Headquarters. It*

bothered me because it soon became apparent that each time we attacked, the enemy was waiting for us. [2]

We could, of course, have won the Korean War, but victory was not the goal of the UN officials who manipulated events. I did not realize it at the time, but the United Nation structure makes sure that the undersecretary of the Security Council who was responsible for military matters is always from the Soviet bloc. [3]

Importance Of The Vietnam War

America again suffered military defeat in losing the Vietnam War, and a shameful defeat at that. The war was represented by many liberal politicians and the liberal news media as a dishonorable war. We were portrayed as big bullies, enforcing ourselves on a smaller, weaker nation for our own gain. It did not seem to occur to them to question what could we possibly gain from a little backward country with no significant resources. This long war, ending in ignominious defeat, served American Marxist ends in two very major ways.

1. The war had a profound effect on public confidence in the "goodness" of America and in our military. We were very specifically made to feel guilty and ashamed of our country. Our resolve and confidence to get involved in another war with Communists was shaken; we should learn our lesson and not take them on again. Politicians still talk of not getting ourselves bogged down in "another Vietnam."

2. The war expended $140 billion, consuming most of our defense budget *without adding a thing to our strategic capability or in an any way increasing our ability to face the Soviet threat.*

AMERICA'S "NO-WIN" POLICY

By intent, the American military was not allowed to win the Vietnam War. It may not have started out that way, when most Americans were genuinely concerned about stopping the spread of the brutality of Communism in Asia, but under presidents Johnson and Nixon, it quickly became that way. Throughout the war America kept trying to get the Communists to the negotiating table so that a "coalition government" could be established (the usual pattern for a Communist take-over, as we have seen). However, the Communists were not willing. Why should they be, as long as the Americans clearly showed they had no intention of winning the war? *US News and World Report* observed that, "While North Vietnam, the bastion of the enemy, is spared the suffering—spared the serious destruction, they have no motive to end the war."[4]

In a "semi-official" glimpse into the thinking of our policy bureaucrats, the Assistant Secretary of Defense wrote the following in answer to a father who had lost his only son in the war and wanted to know why he died:

> *We are engaged in a limited war for limited objectives. Our military actions must be weighed against those limited objectives. Our bombing operations in the North are conducted within certain constraints because they are tied to limited political objectives in the South...we are not seeking to destroy the government of North Vietnam.* [5]

Small comfort to a bereaved father! No noble or patriotic reason given here; just political mumbo-jumbo. The father must surely have wondered *what were* those "limited objectives" for which his son had died; *why* were the forces his son fought with "constrained;" *why are we not seeking to destroy the enemy that killed his son.*

Military Restrictions

The American military was restricted from doing what was necessary to win the war. This was so obvious that a 1966 *US News and World Report* stated:

> *Bombing by the US of North Vietnam remains rigidly limited . . . The power of the US is totally throttled; naval power is not used, while supplies flow freely to the enemy; air power is barely used and denied the right to attack any key industries, key power sites, key supply areas . . . Military leaders of course want to change all this—to fight the war with all we have. The political leaders bar that. They take a sophisticated approach, using a little military with a lot of politics.* [6]

Politicians running the war established "rules of engagement" with "no fire" zones which could prohibit American soldiers from firing unless fired upon. Then many times the Americans were prohibited from holding onto their gains. Ground would be taken from the enemy, and they would be ordered to withdraw. Then they would be ordered to retake it!

For example, in one operation in May of 1967, two divisions of American Marines moved into an area south of the Demilitarized Zone, clearing it of invading North Vietnamese at the cost of 119 Americans killed and 817 wounded. They were then ordered to retreat. Then a few days later, they were ordered to re-take the same area and were ambushed, killing 93 more Marines and wounding another 309. Again, they were ordered to withdraw. Three weeks later, another battalion was sent into the same area, and 23 more men were killed and 191 wounded. The St. Globe Democrat said, "It is this constant fighting and taking casualties for ground that is never held that lies behind the growing criticism of the official strategy." [7]

The Air Force was also restricted. American pilots were specifically prohibited from attacking airplanes and supplies that were on the ground awaiting disbursement to the battle field. A member of the Preparedness Committee, Senator Stuart Symington, visited Vietnam. One pilot told the Senator that he was prohibited from attacking barges loaded with trucks, ammunition and oil which had been unloaded from Soviet ships. He said that he would have to risk his life destroying the trucks one at a time as they traveled down the Ho Chi Minh Trail. He asked the Senator, "Is not a North Vietnamese barge loaded with weapons and ammunition a legitimate military target?" [8]

Another pilot told the Senator he was forbidden to attack and destroy Russian MIG-21 fighter planes when they were vulnerable on the ground at their base near Hanoi. He was only allowed to attack them after they had taken off and were attacking him (under the "Rules of Engagement"). The commander of the US 7th Air Force, Major General John B. Lavelle was fired in 1972 and sent home for ordering air strikes against North Vietnamese airfields, missiles, and artillery. The strikes violated rules prohibiting all "protective reaction" strikes into North Vietnam. Lavelle said he ordered the strikes, "after his pilots saw and photographed a five-month buildup of Soviet built MIG jet fighters at three airfields just across the demilitarized zone, along with SAM missile sites, heavy 133 mm artillery guns, antiaircraft guns and tanks." Although he had not received official authorization for the strikes, he believed he did not exceed his authority, saying, "At that time, as a commander on the spot concerned with the safety of my men, and at the same time trying to stop the buildup that was being made for Hanoi's invasion of the South, I felt that these were justifiable actions." [9]

And the American military was restricted from going into neighboring Cambodia, where the Viet Cong and North Vietnamese could then operate unhindered by American troops or air strikes, moving their men and supplies without fear of harm, and a place to retreat to when needed.

After President Nixon was elected in 1968 (on a platform of ending the war in Vietnam), he ordered the bombing of Cambodian sanctuaries in 1970, and it appeared that at last we were getting serious about winning the war. However, a defecting, high-ranking North Vietnamese army officer later revealed that the Communists had all the details of the bombing well in advance, and in fact knew about *all* allied military operations in Vietnam! A newspaper story on it had the headline, Cambodia Was No Secret. When the Americans bombed Cambodia, the Communists had moved their men and materials safely out of harm's way.

The Pentagon made sure to keep the Communists officially informed on what targets the Americans would and would not hit. For example, in September 1967, American airplanes attacked a Communist facility near the port of Haiphong. Some newspapers interpreted the attack to mean that our ban on bombing the port itself had been overruled. [10] Two days later, Washington officially notified the North Vietnamese that the port of Haiphong would be safe from attack. The Associated Press reported, "The Pentagon, in its eagerness to show that Secretary of Defense Robert S. McNamara was not overruled in recent war decisions, has given North Vietnam official word that port facilities of Haiphong are safe from attack at present."[11]

Sellout To Defeat

It is a shocking truth that those who shaped America's operating policy—Democratic or Republican—had no serious intention of keeping South Vietnam from a Communist takeover. In fact, quite the opposite. From time to time the government made statements that revealed their real intentions, such as the headlines:

LBJ's Aide Says Red May be in New South Vietnamese Regime. [12]

And Nixon's Presidential Aide, Henry Kissinger, saying "The United States would not be opposed to a peaceful Communist takeover in Vietnam."[13]

Statements such as these prepared the American public for what was coming. It is unfortunate that very few wondered why our servicemen were dying by the tens of thousands to keep North Vietnam Communists out of South Vietnam, if our government was not opposed to a "peaceful" Communist takeover! *For what were they dying?!*

Finally, after twelve years of war, America pulled out of South Vietnam and virtually handed it over to the North Vietnam Communists. In pulling out, America cut back essential military supplies to South Vietnam and left them to fight alone. A *Washington Post* article reported, "The US has cut its supplies of artillery and heavy weapons ammunition to Saigon's armed forces . . . in an attempt to reduce the overall level of violence in Vietnam, according to authoritative sources." [14]

We were making sure the North Vietnamese could complete their takeover. The final outcome became inevitable. Cutting desperately needed military supplies to an embattled army does *not* reduce the level of violence. It ensures their violent destruction, which is exactly what happened. The North Vietnamese overwhelmed the South and it was all over. Headlines read:

SOUTH VIETNAM SURRENDERS UNCONDITIONALLY TO REDS [15]

The American government actively facilitated the very thing that over 58,000 American soldiers died to supposedly prevent.

ROLE OF THE MEDIA

The American government could not have pulled off their brilliant defeat in Vietnam without the help of the American liberal news media. Journalist Allan Brownfield, in a special report entitled *"How Media Bias Distorts Our View of the World"* wrote,

> *The Vietnam War, many believe, was lost, not on the battlefield, but on the home front. The Viet Cong was portrayed in the media, not as a Communist army supported and controlled by Ho Chi Minh and the North Vietnamese, but as "nationalists" who only wanted a better life and independence.* [16]

The Communists launched a massive military campaign in South Vietnam in January and February of 1968 called the Tet Offensive. In 1982, a former Communist Vietnamese official said that the offensive was catastrophic to them, costing over one half of their forces. However, it was reported by the news media as a brilliant Communist victory, which was an outright lie. What really happened was purposefully suppressed. Arnaud De Borchgrave, a senior editor at *Newsweek*, was assigned to Saigon at the time of the Tet offensive. In a White House meeting later, in 1986, he told how his reports from Saigon were handled by *Newsweek*. His comments were reported in an account of the meeting published by *Accuracy in Media*,

> *[T]he Vietcong Tet offensive had been an unmitigated disaster for them. (Borchgrave) said that Osborne Elliott, then the editor-in-chief of Newsweek... declared that it was the consensus of the senior editors of Newsweek that we had lost the war and that we should get out. Borchgrave said: "My file from Saigon reported just the opposite, and not one word of what I filed got (into) Newsweek."* [17]

In another major campaign, the Battle of He San, US Marines were deployed to block a major advance by the North Vietnamese army. In a battle, superbly executed by Marine forces, the Air Force and South Vietnamese soldiers over 12,000 North Vietnamese were killed in 77 days of combat with a loss of 205 Marines. It was a crushing defeat for the North Vietnamese. However, it was represented in the American media as a hopeless siege which could only end in disaster. [18]

Reporter Peter Braestrup documented how the American media turned this massive Communist defeat into a political defeat for the United States:

Rarely has contemporary-crisis journalism turned out, in retrospect, to have veered so widely from reality. Essentially, the dominant themes of the words and film from Vietnam added up to a portrait of defeat for the allies. Historians, on the contrary, have concluded that the Tet Offensive resulted in a severe military setback for Hanoi in the South. [19]

After the war, when the head of the Communist South Vietnamese Republic, Nguen Huu Tho, visited Moscow, he commented on the Communist triumph, saying:

Victories were won in the first place by the resolute and energetic struggle of our own people, determined on freedom and sovereignty; by the effective aid of the Socialist countries, and by the efforts of the world's progressive and peaceful people including those in the United States . . . who have given moral and political aid to our just struggles. [20]

COULD WE HAVE WON THE WAR?

When the Air Force Chief of Staff Gen. John McConnell was asked by a reporter if it were true that we could win this war, he said, "Of course it's true . . . we could achieve this victory overnight. We could simply destroy North Vietnam. President Johnson has emphasized that we are to keep this conflict at the lowest possible level of intensity for humanitarian as well as political reasons." [21]

What General McConnell said was true. The war could have been brought to an absolute stand-still with a few well-placed, bombs and little loss of life. Eighty percent of the Communist's war supplies came through Haiphong Harbor, an unnatural harbor whose channel had to be continually dredged. Most of the rest was manufactured in the Hanoi area, much of which depends on an extensive dyke system to keep the Red River from flooding it. An air raid sinking a vessel in the harbor channel would indefinitely prevent supplies from coming into the harbor. A few more bombs breaching the dyke system protecting Hanoi, would flood the area and bring a lot of manufacturing to a standstill. Without supplies, the Communist military machine would have simply ground to a halt. [22]

THE AFTERMATH

After the war, countless South Vietnamese started to "vote with their feet" as they always do in countries taken over by Communists. They frantically tried to escape from the atrocities, purges and suffering which will always follow as the Communists eliminate every conceivable threat to their new regime and the ransacking of society. Absolute terror reigned. Where was the liberal news media then? They never report what *really* happens when the Communists take over? The fact is, they do not care about the cost—they care only that their cause has been advanced.

And what was the cost of America's pullout? ***In the first two years following the fall of Saigon, there were almost twice as many deaths in the resulting purges than from the entire ten years of the Vietnam War.***[23]

In light of this, recall how our government had muzzled our military, kept the conflict at the lowest possible level and withheld defensive arms and supplies to South Vietnam supposedly for *"humanitarian reasons"* and to *"reduce the overall level of violence."* ***It is virtually impossible to suppose that our leaders and policy makers did not know what was going to happen.*** It was simply a repeat of what had happened many times before, starting with Russia, where millions were killed to establish and maintain the reign of terror. ***What happened in Vietnam was an inevitable repeat of history.***

As a result of the take-over, countless thousands of South Vietnamese cast themselves adrift in small boats on the South China Sea to escape. Headlines reported; BETTER TO DIE AT SEA THAN LIVE UNDER COMMUNISM.[24] They would rather take the remote chance of being picked up on the high seas than live in a so-called Communist workers "paradise"!

President Nixon, toward the end of the war in 1973, assured the war-weary American nation that the war "has all been worthwhile." Then, as the war finally ended in 1974, when the sellout was complete, he told the nation that we "today have concluded an agreement to end the war and bring peace with honor in Vietnam and in Southeast Asia."[25] Those who know what really happened would strongly object to referring to the outcome as "peace with honor."

CHAPTER 7

THE RESULTING BALANCE
OF POWER

THE REVEALING NUMBERS

As a result of America appeasing the Soviets and ensuring they surpassed us militarily, the balance of power changed from that of overwhelming American superiority in 1960 to one of critical inferiority in 1980, when it looked like the following.

TABLE 1: STRATEGIC MISSILE DEPLOYMENT, CIVILIAN VULNERABILITY

	USA	USSR
Ratio Of Total Missile Payload For All ICBMs And SLBMs [A]	1	3.5
Ratio Of Total Missile Warhead Explosive Power	1	5
Average Warhead Size, Megatons (Mt)[B]	0.2	1.2
Number Of ABMs And SAMs [C] Deployed For Strategic Defense	0	9,300
Industrial Workers Protected By Nuclear Fallout Bunkers	0	60 million
Estimated Civilian Casualties In An All-Out Nuclear War[D]	140-160 million	10-20 million

Strategic weapons are those intended to strike the essential military targets and/or civilian population and infrastructure of an enemy

[A] Inter-Continental Ballistic Missiles; Submarine Launched Ballistic Missiles

[B] Equivalent millions of tons of conventional high explosive (TNT)

[C] Anti-Ballistic Missiles and Surface-to-Air Missiles

[D] Estimate from various sources[1]

Appendix III gives the detailed numbers upon which this summary is based and their documented source.

TABLE 2: TACTICAL CONVENTIONAL FORCES

	USA	USSR
Ratio Of Active Military Personnel	1	2.3
Ratio Of Ready Reserve Military Personnel	1	7.3
Ratio Of Heavy And Medium Battle Tanks	1	4.4
Ratio Of Heavy Artillery	1	4.7
Ratio Of Tactical Aircraft	1	1.5

Tactical forces are those used in battle-field situations against enemy military forces.

AMERICA WAS WARNED

America Was Warned By Retired Military Leaders

In January 1979, a group of 170 retired generals and admirals signed an open letter to President Jimmy Carter pointing out America's vulnerable military position and virtually *pleaded* with him to restore America's declining military strength in light of Soviet increasing strength and obvious resolve to defeat the West. This open letter was published as a full-page ad in The New York Times and other newspapers around the nation. Following are some excerpts from that letter:

> *The National Intelligence Estimate, the most authoritative US government evaluation of intelligence data, acknowledges at last that the Soviet Union is heading for superiority—not parity—in the military arena. This represents a complete reversal of official judgments that were a substantial factor in allowing our government to pursue detente and overall accommodation with the Soviet regime.*
>
> *By any criteria, the increasing Soviet challenge to America's position in global affairs is manifest:*
>
> *– While the US has developed only one ICBM system since 1965, the USSR has developed seven.*
>
> *– In addition to modernizing its ICBM systems, the Soviet Union has invested heavily in additional submarine-launched ballistic missiles (SLBMs).*
>
> *– The Backfire bomber, the newest addition to the Soviet Union's strategic arsenal, launched from Arctic bases, is capable of delivering weapons anywhere in the US without refueling.*
>
> *– Advances in Soviet MIRV technology are overcoming rapidly whatever lead we had in quality and quantity of warheads; the dramatic development in Soviet naval power matching the modernization of Soviet air and ground*

forces now threatens US security in vital sea lanes providing access to essential resources.

Soviet defense literature explicitly rejects the Western doctrine of "Mutually Assured Destruction." It rejects specifically the notion that nuclear war means suicide. Soviet forces are structured to fight, survive and win nuclear war. We urge you, Mr. President, to bring these facts to the attention of our fellow citizens so that all Americans will understand the dimension of the Soviet military challenge . . . .

Clearly, moreover, we must restore the global military balance at both the strategic and conventional levels, or neither we nor our allies will be able to defuse the Soviet challenge. Our diplomacy will have little meaning and our search for peace will be futile unless we can demonstrate the necessary political will and military credibility to press effectively for peaceful co-existence based upon balance of power between East and West, between Israel and its Arab neighbors, between our friends and Russia's clients in Africa and Asia . . .

We urge you, Mr. President, *to make our pursuit of genuine peace realistic and effective by moving now to restore the global military balance and America's credibility as a leader of the Free World . . .*

We urge you, Mr. President, to desist from any new arms control agreement that would threaten to perpetuate the current strategic imbalance and reinforce permanent Soviet strategic superiority...

For America and the world, *we urge you, Mr. President, to lead in building a coalition for genuine peace in cooperation with the NATO nations, Japan, Israel and other proven friends and allies who share our commitment to freedom and human dignity.*

Respectfully yours,
(Signed by 170 US retired generals and admirals)[2]

The American public heard the truth of the precarious state of our national security from men with impeccable qualifications who knew the facts of our real military position better than anyone else. Their impassioned plea to the President cut through all the deception and hypocrisy of our national leaders—those charged with the responsibility of defending our nation and our liberty. This plea dramatically revealed they had a profoundly different idea of what was best for America based on traditional American patriotism and military reality. That this public plea had no effect on our leaders, produced no public outcry, is witness to the apathetic, state of the American public, and the dogged determination of our leaders to cast ourselves upon the "good mercies" of an enemy dedicated to bringing us down.

America Was Warned From Within The Soviet Union

The West should have been warned by an internal speech made by Soviet premier Brezhnev in Prague in 1973 to Communist Party officials. Somehow the contents of the speech got out and it was reported in several American newspapers. Brezhnev said that through detente they would achieve what their predecessors had been unable to with the "mailed fist" He told them,

> *Trust us, comrades, for by 1985 . . . we will have achieved most of our objectives in Western Europe. We will have improved our economy. And a decisive shift in the correlation of forces will be such that, come 1985, we will be able to extend our will wherever we need to.*[3]

This should have created a storm, but it was ignored. Soviet exile Vladimir Bukovsky, who was released from a Soviet political prison to the West in exchange for a leading Communist held in a Western prison, commented on Brezhnev's speech in an interview with *National Review* in April 1977.

> *I was not at all surprised by Brezhnev's statement. But what does surprise me is the fact that politicians in the West can't seem to understand what he's talking about. Western politicians simply don't understand the psychology of Brezhnev, the psychology of the Soviet leaders.*[4]

CHAPTER 8

THE COLD WAR FORMALLY ENDS

THE COLLAPSE OF THE SOVIET UNION

By the mid to late 1980s the Soviet Union and Eastern Europe were in trouble. Their economies were in shambles and in some areas their people were close to open rebellion. The Soviets were spending so much on their massive military buildup to defeat America that they could not feed their own people. Ruthless repression, plus "timely" economic aid from America had saved the Soviet Union from collapse more than once in the past. Would we save them again?

President Reagan's Berlin Wall Speech

President Ronald Reagan was the first Cold War era president who had the fortitude to publicly call the Soviet Union what it really was—*evil!* [1] He believed the Soviet empire could, and should, be brought to an end. Reagan's aim regarding the Soviet Union was not agreement, but victory. At one point, he said the "ultimate goal of American foreign policy is not just the prevention of war but the extension of freedom—to see that every nation, every people, every person someday enjoy the blessings of liberty." [2]

In a key speech that contributed to the Soviet collapse, President Reagan gave one of the great liberty speeches of history as he stood by the Berlin Wall on June 12, 1987. He boldly compared the economic freedom of capitalism that had transformed the rubble of post-war West Berlin into a thriving prosperous city, with the failed, backward state of the Communist world that could not even feed itself. He linked prosperity to freedom. Following are some excerpts from his speech:

In the Communist world, we see failure, technological backwardness, declining standards of health, even want of the most basic kind—too little food. Even today, the Soviet Union still cannot feed itself. After these four decades, then, there stands before the entire world one great and inescapable conclusion: Freedom leads to prosperity!

Reagan then acknowledged the possible stirring of freedom coming from the Soviet leaders, but he questioned their motives:

And now the Soviets themselves may, in a limited way, be coming to understand the importance of freedom. We hear much from Moscow about a new policy of reform and openness . . . Are these the beginnings of profound changes in the Soviet state? Or are they token gestures, intended to raise false hopes in the West, or to strengthen the Soviet system without changing it? We welcome change and openness; for we believe that freedom and security go together, that the advance of human liberty can only strengthen the cause of world peace.

Then, in the highlight of the speech, President Reagan issued a bold, daring challenge to the Soviet leader, Mikhail Gorbachev:

There is one sign the Soviets can make that would be unmistakable, that would advance dramatically the cause of freedom and peace. General Secretary Gorbachev, if you seek peace, if you seek prosperity for the Soviet Union and Eastern Europe, if you seek liberalization: Come here to this gate! Mr. Gorbachev, open this gate! Mr. Gorbachev, tear down this wall! [3]

The response of Berliners was electric! It was quietly mirrored by the oppressed people of Eastern Europe. Finally—a man with the strength of character and belief in liberty who had the "guts" to publicly and boldly demand of the Soviet leader that if he meant what he said about peace, he should tear down the wall that kept his people locked in, and kept freedom out.

Needless to say, the Marxist-minded bureaucrats of the State Department were horrified. History Professor Douglas Brinkley describes what the reaction of the State Department had been to the circulated draft of the speech (by White House speech writer, Peter Robinson), and how Reagan decided to give the speech anyway.

"America's top foreign policy experts were vehement that Reagan not deliver the so-called crude and unduly provocative speech, which would only incite friction with the Kremlin. Even on the morning that Reagan arrived in

Berlin, top aides pleaded with the president not to deliver the Robinson speech. Reagan told his top advisers that he would consider their recommendation. But on the limousine ride to the Brandenburg Gate, Reagan told his deputy chief of staff, Ken Duberstein that he just had to deliver the powerful line about tearing down the wall. With an 'aw shucks' smile, he poked Duberstein in the ribs and said, 'The boys at State are going to kill me, but it's the right thing to do.'" [4]

THE CLOSING STAGES OF THE SOVIET EMPIRE

Reagan's stand against Communism was a tremendous encouragement to the enslaved peoples of Eastern Europe. Liberty began to stir. After the Solidarity Labor movement in Poland challenged Soviet authority, social unrest quickened all over Eastern Europe. Soviet Premier Gorbachev made dramatic changes, agreeing to reduce Soviet military strength, free the enslaved nations of Europe, and stop exporting revolution and bloodshed around the world.

The Soviets adopted a policy they called glasnost ("openness"), claiming they wanted world peace and had no plans for conquest. In return, the United States and Western nations agreed to help rebuild the Soviet economy on a free-enterprise model. Yes, Russia was again going to get desperately needed economic aid from America! The Soviets called this plan Perestroika ("restructuring").

As a result, the Soviets began withdrawing troops, and the hopes of the Eastern European nations rose. *Realizing that their move for freedom would not be crushed,* they demanded release from their Communist yoke. Unrest spread on the Soviet bloc.

Toward the end of 1989, the people of Poland, Hungary, East Germany, Czechoslovakia, and Romania rose up and overthrew their Communist leaders. Then the Berlin Wall was knocked down and millions of Berliners—East and West—took to the streets to celebrate. (The wall came down on November 9, 1989, less than 2 1/2 years after President Reagan's famous "tear down this wall" speech.)

When the Soviet Union finally collapsed, Russia declared herself to be an independent nation in 1991 and other former Soviet republics followed. However, by the end of 1991, twelve of the former fifteen Soviet republics had joined together to form another union, the Commonwealth of Independent States CIS).

WAS THE SOVIET COLLAPSE "ALLOWED" TO HAPPEN?

The question arises, was the collapse real? Was it genuine in that the Soviet leaders were really forced out of office, "going down in flames" so to speak? Or was it pre-planned and staged, with all the *appearance* of a genuine collapse? We have to admit that the latter would be in keeping with the nature and character of Soviet leadership. As we noted in the Preface, it is hard to imagine them giving up without having something up their sleeves. Those who understand the unchangeable, "never-die" nature of Communism know this was not an irreversible admission of defeat. And the Soviet collapse could well have been the application of Lenin's advice, "It is necessary sometimes to take one step backward so we may take two steps forward." A big step backwards to be sure, but perhaps one that would eventually open the door to bringing down the West!

Unless they totally gave up on their whole plan and purpose of the previous 85 years, the Soviet goal and its relentless drive would rise again. After careful planning and manipulation, Russia could be expected to gradually reestablish Soviet-like political control and modernize their military. At the right time, they would make their move, starting with the take-over of former key areas of the old Soviet Union (like Crimea and Ukraine). They would want America to be in a much weakened, unsuspecting state, consumed with other problems. And it would help immeasurably if they were again under corrupt, unpatriotic leadership who had little or no regard for traditional American liberty and patriotic values, and who shamelessly appeased their enemies.

It has to be remembered that Reagan's Strategic Defense Initiative (SDI) was a direct threat to Soviet plans. This was a high-tech missile defense system proposed in 1983 to very effectively protect the United States from strategic nuclear missile attack. It combined ground-based units and orbital deployment platforms, disdainfully referred to in the liberal media as "Star Wars." Reagan was a strong critic of Mutual Assured Destruction, and knew the vital need to defend ourselves!

Even before SDI, the Soviet Union and Eastern Europe were facing increasing economic problems and social unrest. They were locked into their plans for military conquest, spending so much on their massive military buildup that in some areas economic conditions were bringing the people to the point of rebellion.

It is highly significant that the Soviets did not back off in their military spending to ease the economic plight of their people, or in any way try to placate them. Neither did they come down hard to crush the impending outbreaks, as they had in the past. *They were making no serious effort to avert a disastrous break-up of their empire.*

In conjunction with an atmosphere of detente, an allowed, covertly encouraged, managed "collapse" could well be a master-move to assure eventual victory for the Soviet cause. It would:

1. Calm the unrest among the Soviet people, giving them hope for change in their economic plight, and restore a measure of stability;
2. Obtain another "wave" of desperately needed economic assistance from the West to save their economy, opening the door to hand-outs and advantageous trade with them;
3. Give America the confidence to disarm. This became increasing more important because of SDI, which terrified the Soviets. They knew they could not match our technology. A spirit of detente and a staged "collapse" of the Soviet Union would remove any reason for America to build SDI. (And it did!);
4. Gain international respectability for Russian leaders as men who really have changed and want to cooperate with the West, so they could receive all kinds of political and economic concessions.

As it turns out, there is much evidence to suggest that a covert, internally managed "collapse" of the Soviet empire had been planned for some time. There is the testimony of high-ranking officials who defected to the West. *And,* there is much to be seen in the political scene after the collapse that would confirm that the collapse had been pre-planned and staged, or purposefully allowed to happen.

The Testimony Of Defectors

At least three defectors informed the West that the Kremlin had a long range strategy of deception on a massive scale. Two of them (Jan Sejna and Anatoliy Golitsyn) told us that the plan involved the controlled collapse of Soviet Russia's military alliance in Eastern Europe, the Warsaw Pact.[5]

Former top KGB planner, Anatoliy Golitsyn, who defected to the West in 1961 began warning the West in 1982 of a coming period of false liberalization in the USSR, apparent independence for the Communist nations of Eastern Europe, and the reunification of Germany. In his book *New Lies for Old* he wrote:

> *Communist strategists are now poised to enter into the final, offensive phase of their long-range policy . . . for the complete triumph of Communism . . . Among such previously unthinkable strategies are the introduction of false liberalization in Eastern Europe and, probably, in the Soviet Union, and the exhibition of spurious independence on the part of regimes in Romania Czechoslovakia and Poland.*[6]

In 1990, Golitsyn described further how the "liberalized" Soviet Union would operate:

The Communists have succeeded in concealing from the West that the non-Communist parties [within the former USSR] are secret partners, not alternatives or rivals, and that the new power structures, though they have democratic form, are in reality more pliable and effective structures introduced and guided by Communist parties with a broader base. Because of this Communist control, they are not true democracies and cannot become so in the future . . . they are a new generation of revolutionaries who are using "democratic" reforms as a new way to achieve final victory. [7]

Understandably, there has been considerable controversy over Golitsyn's claims, even though almost all the 130 predictions he made in 1982 had been fulfilled by 1990, including the demolition of the Berlin Wall and the reunification of Germany.

The Political Scene Since The Soviet Collapse

Whether or not the collapse was managed, there is no questioning the fact that in these countries, there has been no real ideological change, except for some "window dressing." The political and military situation in Russia and other former Soviet Union states, up to the present day, strongly supports the contention of a staged collapse.

Western democracy and capitalism have not been installed in Russia. Private property ownership, in the Western sense, does not really exist. The people do not understand the philosophy of a free society. They believe that the "state" should provide for them, and while it failed to do so under communism, under the new system, they expect it would. For seventy four years they had been thoroughly instilled with the belief that the state owns all things; is the measure of all things; and is responsible for all things. Mikhail Gorbachev (president of the USSR when it collapsed) made it very clear in his book *Perestroika* that the policies of Glasnost and Perestroika are *not* based on Western ideas of democracy, but on raw Socialism:

To put an end to all the rumors and speculations that abound in the West about this, I would like to point out once again that we are conducting all out reforms in accordance with the socialist choice. We are looking within socialism, rather than outside of it, for the answers to all the questions that arise. We assess our successes and errors alike by socialist standards. Those who hope we shall move away from the socialist path will be greatly disappointed. Every part of our program of perestroika — and the program as a whole, for that matter – is fully based on the principle of more socialism and more democracy."[8]

The people of the former Soviet states still fear and distrust the Capitalist system. Their distrust is being fed by the Russian government's present-day anti-American propaganda, and by what they see on television of what American society is now like (the consequences of the destructive "long march" through its institutions by the radicalized left). The Russian people are looking more and more on America as representing what they do *not* want to be, and as an enemy.

While there was a name change from Communism to Socialism in the former Soviet bloc countries, over 90 percent of the former Communist power structure remained in place. Their underlying Communists philosophy was never renounced. Political power and the control of society remained centralized in the hands of the State. The free enterprise system of privatization was mostly talked about; there were few real, tangible changes.

The Military Scene Since The Soviet Collapse

During the period leading up to the end of the Cold War, the Soviets were out-producing the United States in the production of ICBMs by over 18 to 1; SLBMs by over 2 to 1 and submarine launched cruise missiles by 11 to 1.[9] Although Gorbachev instigated the policies of detente, glasnost, and perestroika and spoke about peace, cooperation, and change, the relentless Soviet military buildup continued after the "collapse." The key, unanswered question is "WHY the continued build-up of their military?" It was obvious they were no longer threatened by America and the West, who were rushing in to restore their economy and help them back on to their feet.

The question worried US Defense Secretary Dick Cheney, who, in late 1991, when the Communist Party had supposedly been dissolved, expressed concern about the former Soviet Republic's continued production and deployment of nuclear weapons despite their commitments to reduce them. He noted,

> *One of the things I'm concerned about is that we still see, even at this late date with their economy in a state of utter collapse . . . efforts inside the former Soviet Union to produce more weapons, to deploy new ballistic missiles against the United States.*[10]

However, nothing was done about his concern, and the key question of "WHY" was not investigated or answered. It could be argued, "why should we care? We won the Cold War, right? We should therefore not be too concerned about Russia continuing to develop new generations of key strategic weapons. Never mind that in recent years, while in the midst of severe domestic economic problems, they have spent an incredible amount of money developing new generations of strategic offensive and defensive weapons. They have aggressively developed surface-to-air missiles, cruise missiles, ICBMs and SLBMs that are one or more generations more advanced than our own. And their latest fighter aircraft are a match for the best America has. Surely they can't be thinking of actually *using* all this advanced firepower! Blackmail perhaps? Attack or blackmail who?

Dedicated Marxists have never given up their goal of world-wide communism. Who stands most in their way?

In addition to what is going on in Russia right now, Communism and Marxism have certainly not died in the rest of the world. Over one billion people are still under Communism in China, as well as other nations such as North Korea and Vietnam, and South America is becoming a Communist sphere.

CHAPTER 9

HOW DID AMERICA SURVIVE?

THE NATURE OF AMERICA'S LEADERSHIP

What Motivated Those Who Betrayed Us?

What motivates people to take over their government and betray their country by aiding and abetting its enemies? How could they justify it? Just who were these men?

We can identify three classes of people who were involved. While they had different reasons for their betrayal, they had certain fundamental beliefs in common. First and foremost, they did not understand liberty—upon what it was founded, what it has cost and why it is so precious. They had total disregard for individual liberty as something to be preserved and defended at all cost. None of them would have joined that great American patriot Patrick Henry in saying, "Give me liberty or give me death!" They had little or no understanding or appreciation of America's Christian heritage and the principles upon which this nation was founded, and which made it great. And they certainly did not have the faith of our Founding Fathers, believing in the living God who was providentially involved in the birth of our nation.

As can be seen from the summary of their prevailing worldview (Appendix I), they all had a Socialist mindset, believing in a centralized government that planned and controlled the economy and the running of society. And they all believed in globalism. It should be noted here that the threat of international Communism was an essential factor in the promotion of a global government. Dr. Lincoln Bloomfield, who has been member of the US State Department, National Security Council and professor of Political Science at MIT, has said, "If the Communist dynamic was greatly abated, the West might lose whatever incentive it has for world *government.*" [1]

Before we look more specifically into the three categories into which we can divide these people, comment should be made on the need to sometimes be blunt and call people what they really are. Not to put them down personally, but to expose the nature of those who have treasonably betrayed us. I hope this will not be seen as un-Christian. Our Lord pulled no punches in calling hypocritical Pharisees "white-washed tombs—clean and white on the outside, but full of corruption on the inside." He was exposing the leaders of the time, which is what we are talking about here.

The first category consisted of those who sincerely believed (or blindly hoped) that Communists would "mellow" and change in their determination to conquer and rule the world, who simply had to be given time to eventually come to their senses, give up their dictatorial ways and become good, solid, friendly neighbors. They had little or no ideological problems with Communists, basically trusting them. They viewed their lying and deceptions as simply "normal politics" (as politicians, they did the same themselves!). They were predictable and easily manipulated. Lenin is credited with describing people like this as *"USEFUL IDIOTS"* for the Marxist cause.

Second, there were those who were literally scared senseless by the strength and brutality of the Soviet system. They were the "better red than dead" crowd who were perfectly willing to roll over and surrender without a whimper. They would sell out their country and our liberty in a heart-beat—whatever it took to ensure they could live. They had nothing outside of themselves worth standing up for, nothing worth fighting for, *and certainly nothing in life worth dying for.* These were also "useful idiots," but they were more. They were *COWARDS.*

Third, there were those who would infinitely prefer to live in a collectivist, Marxist-Communist society than a Christian-Capitalist one. They hated America because they hated what America has traditionally stood for, believing that Capitalism and old-time Christianity are inherently evil. They would stop at nothing to destroy the system into which they were born, and which allowed them the freedom to believe and say whatever they wanted. To patriotic Americans, these people were outright *TRAITORS.*

Americans had no idea their country was in the hands of "idiots," "cowards," and "traitors!" If they had, they would have thrown them out of office. The evidence of what was happening was certainly there. Our nation's Founding Fathers warned future Americans that "the price of liberty is eternal vigilance." The sad fact is that Americans have taken their liberty for granted and just couldn't be bothered with vigilance. What an absolute tragedy!

George Washington called the attempted betrayal and sellout of our country and our cause to the British by Benedict Arnold "treason of the blackest dye."

At least England was our "motherland" and a nominally Christian nation. What would Washington call those who would sell us out to a brutal, atheistic, Christian-killing, Marxist dictatorship?

Did Our Leaders Really Know What They Were Doing?

Our leaders were certainly not gullible fools (as some have made them out to be). They knew the Soviets were becoming stronger and less vulnerable while we steadily and purposefully reduced our strength and made sure our cities were totally vulnerable. They also knew the ABM and SALT treaties were being flagrantly violated, and they willfully ignored it. *The real movers and shakers of American policy knew exactly what they were doing.* Phyllis Schlafly and Rear Admiral Chester Ward commented on one of them:

> *Take the outstanding case of Robert Stranger McNamara. Nearly every one of the retired members of the Joint Chiefs of Staff and senior military commanders who spoke out . . . [demonstrate] conclusively, on the basis of evidence and expertise, that all McNamara's major policies were "wrong," "mistaken," "dangerous," and "based on false and foolish premises." Our military experts have proved that all McNamara's programs led to reducing US strategic military power, even rendering US tactical military power ineffective, as in Vietnam. Congressional committee reports have proved the same. Sometimes, McNamara's critics go so far as to charge him with "deceit," but that is all. The fact is, that McNamara is a brilliant man who had a definite objective, and who never made a major mistake in his efforts to achieve it. **All his policy decisions were completely consistent, and each of them contributed to his overall plan—the destruction of US strategic nuclear striking power.**[2] (Emphasis added)*

To the Western mind, these people were carrying out the most irresponsible, criminally chargeable acts of treason and betrayal seen in any civilized government charged with the defense of its own people. But, not so to the Marxist mind!

By now it should be clear that *the actions of our leaders paralleled the Marxist worldview.* They acted as if they *wanted* America to be totally vulnerable to the Soviets; as if they *wanted* the Soviet Union to be sovereign over them; as if they *wanted* America to disarm, give up *its* sovereignty and be transformed from a Western, Christian, Capitalist state into a servile Communist one. We have to ask, if something quacks like a duck, waddles like a duck and acts like a duck, is it not reasonable to assume it *is* a duck?

WHY AMERICA SURVIVED THE COLD WAR

It is claimed by America's former policy makers and their supporters that our Cold War policy "worked" because nuclear war was prevented. Supposedly, it still would have "worked" even if nuclear war had been averted at the cost of our freedom and national sovereignty. It has been obvious that our leaders were fully prepared to pay that price (if not *hoping* to do so!).

The question then is, did America survive as an undamaged, intact, still-democratic nation *because* of our policy of increasing military weakness, and cowardly appeasement, or *in spite* of it?

Considering America's eventual weakness and vulnerability, and the Soviet's commanding strategic offensive and defensive capacity, what held them back? The Soviet empire was a brutal, absolute dictatorship that had systematically murdered up to 50 million of their own people (estimates vary) to establish and maintain totalitarian control. What could possibly hold them back from killing any number of bitterly hated Christian Capitalists to give them control of the West, which was the only real obstacle they faced in establishing world-wide Communism? Even if the lives of 10-20 million of their own people were at risk, the Soviets had shown that even larger numbers were quite expendable. Their lives were cheap—dirt cheap!

At some point during the late 1980s, the Soviet leader could have called the President of the United States and simply told him that the Soviet army was moving into Western Europe. If American and NATO forces resisted them, the president could watch his totally defenseless cities being annihilated, one by one, until he and the West surrendered unconditionally. America's policy of Mutual Assure Destruction, which only assured our own destruction, had virtually been an *open invitation* to the Soviets to give us this ultimatum! So, why didn't they give it?

What alternatives would the president have apart from surrender? He could order an immediate nuclear attack against fixed Soviet missile silos and military installations, (many of their missiles were mobile-mounted, always moving and could not be targeted), or he could strike Soviet cities and industry. In the former case, the Soviets would launch all their ICBMs as soon as their satellites detected we had launched ours. They would be primed and ready to go before making their phone call. Our missiles would simply hit empty silos, and our cities would then be incinerated.

In the latter case, if we targeted Soviet cities and industry (the worst scenario for the Soviets), some 10 million or so Russians could die—still leaving them a viable nation. (20 million of their citizens died in World War II and they survived.)

In either case, our President would then helplessly watch the total destruction of his own defenseless nation. If faced with such a Soviet ultimatum, it is obvious that the only thing he could do is surrender. The ultimate checkmate.

However, the Soviets had another, and perhaps better option. They could dispense with their phone-call ultimatum, and simply launch a surprise preemptive strike on our ICBM silos and military installations, leaving themselves vulnerable only to our submarine-launched ballistic missiles (SLBMs), *which under our pause policy, we would withhold.* America's liberal leaders have demonstrated over and over their blind faith in negotiations, having infinitely more confidence in the "tongue" than the "sword!" The Soviets would let us know that if we *did* begin an SLBM counter-strike, they would simply proceed with the total destruction of our undefended cities, one by one (or all at once, their choice).

In light of the fact that nothing like this did occur, and America *did* survive the Cold War intact, it would appear that either, for the first time in history, a ruthlessly expanding totalitarian empire was held off by the cowardly appeasement of its weaker, intended victim, or else an act of Providence was involved. To those who would reject the idea of Providence, America's survival has to be seen as the result of our "marvelous" Cold War policy, or it was simply "dumb luck."

It does not take a profound understanding of human nature to know that tyrants and bullies are not stopped by appeasement! They see it as weakness and cowardice (which it usually is) for which they have nothing but contempt. *The only thing they respect is strength.* Weakness invariably encourages them to further their violence.

All things considered, there can only be one reason why the Soviets did not move to take over America and the West (which they were most certainly ready, willing and capable of doing). They had to have been concerned that America *just might* stand up to them and fight. A suicidal fight to be sure, but one that could inflict substantial damage on their military establishments and/or their industrial centers and civilian population. Keep in mind the earlier given estimates of 140-160 million Americans and 10-20 million Soviet citizens killed in an all-out nuclear war. In such a conflict, the Soviet Union would unquestionably survive and be the "last man standing."

But then, given the nature of America's government at the time and their Soviet-appeasing policies, what were the chances that America would fight back? The answer is *virtually zero.* Our leaders *did not want to* fight back—they were more than willing to surrender to the Soviet cause. And the Soviets had to know the kind of people and government they were dealing with. Their agents were everywhere in our government! ***So, all things considered, their restraint can only be realistically explained as an act of Providence.***

During the Cold War-era our government was subverted by a philosophy totally alien to our Christian heritage. In looking back, we ought to be profoundly grateful for the providential preservation of our country, in spite of the corruption and shameful betrayal of our government, and the willful, apathetic blindness of our people.

However, the survival of our national sovereignty was not the only part of the Cold War story. Another facet of American life came out of this era in worse shape than our corrupted government—*our culture*. We need to know what happened.

CHAPTER 10

AMERICA'S CULTURAL REVOLUTION

While our nation's physical integrity and sovereignty survived the Cold War era intact, the Christian basis of our culture did not. We need to go back and see what was happening concurrently with the political deceit and treachery of the era. The political and cultural arenas are not independent, but react intimately with each other. *Both have drastically changed over the last 50 years, forming what our society is today, so they both need to be well understood.*

A cultural revolution is very different from a political one. In a political revolution governments are overthrown, and power changes hands. In a cultural revolution, the very philosophy and principles upon which a society operates—its prevailing values, and the resulting idea of what constitutes a normal, acceptable way of life—are changed. It is a transformation of society itself, not just a change in leadership.

Such a revolution took place in America in the 1960s and 1970s. It has had a cataclysmic effect on every facet of American life. The revolution was planned and initiated by Marxists and executed by a mindless herd of skillfully inflamed and manipulated college students.

The revolution was part of America's sellout to Marxism in the Cold War era, and knowing what happened and why is needed to understand present-day American culture and politics.

THE BASIS OF THE REVOLUTION

A twentieth-century Italian Marxist, Antonio Gramsci, saw that the workers of the West—particularly in America—were not about to rise up in bloody revolution to throw off their Capitalist "oppressors" and install a Marxist government. They enjoyed the highest standard of living in the world and had no intention of giving up their private property and their liberty to the state. Gramsci saw that Marxism could only be installed in the West through the nonviolent but revolutionary destruction and replacement of its culture *from within*.[1]

This process (sometimes called "cultural Marxism") required what Gramsci called "*the long march through the institutions.*" By this he meant the systematic infiltration, subversion, and take-over of all the basic institutions of society—the schools, universities, churches, entertainment and the media—and of course, the political realm. This would start by infusing college and university students with Socialist/Marxist beliefs and values through a liberal/progressive/Socialist/Marxist faculty, which would then gradually spread throughout society. Indoctrinated in this manner, the people would begin to think and act like Marxists, without calling themselves as such. Author Charles Reich described the process in his 1970 book *The Greening of America*:

> *There is a revolution coming. It will not be like the revolutions of the past. It will originate with the individual and with culture, and it would change the political structure only as its final act. It will not require violence to succeed, and it cannot be successfully resisted with violence. It is now spreading with amazing rapidity, and already our laws, institutions, and social structure are changing in consequence . . . This is the revolution of the new generation.*[2]

This revolution has already changed the face of America. The orthodox Communist way of installing Marxism by the violent overthrow of an existing regime and brutalizing its citizens, had been replaced by the far more effective, non-violent method of changing society from within. Such a society would come to believe in the basic tenets of Marxist ideology. It takes decades of patient labor, but anyone familiar with America's history over the past 50 years or so can see that it has been phenomenally successful!

THE STUDENT REVOLT OF THE 1960S[3]

The long march of America's Cultural Revolution began with the student uprisings that swept across college and university campuses in the mid-1960s and early 1970s. Radicalized students seized buildings and issued non-negotiable demands. At Columbia, a dean was held hostage and the office of the college president looted. Similar outrages occurred at campuses, large and small, across the nation. At this point, it is difficult to recapture the suddenness and fury of those insurrections. The nation was totally unprepared.

College administrators were intimidated into totally changing the purpose and function of all levels of modern-day education. Its effect is measured "not in toppled governments, but in shattered values." The totality of the change—the degree to which it has been so astoundingly successful—can be seen by the fact that it has been so largely forgotten. We have changed ourselves so completely, we can no longer perceive the extent of our transformation.[4] In writing about the present-day effect of the sixties culture, political philosopher Harvey Mansfield has noted that:

> *The poison has worked its way into our souls, the effects becoming less visible to us as they become more ordinary. Even those who reject the Sixties unconsciously conceded more than they know to the vicious principle of liberation that once was shouted into the street microphone.*[5]

And what did this revolution produce? Established morality was rejected across the board and unrestrained freedom—unfettered by law, custom, or the promoting of conscience—was glorified. In this shattering of traditional virtues, the fabric of family life has been destroyed. *Broken homes are now the norm in America.* This ideology degrades womanhood and cheapens immeasurably the prevailing view of sexual relations. Casual sexual encounters are now the accepted norm— especially on college campuses ("recreational sex"). It has degraded the media, the entertainment industry, and popular culture to the gutter level. The incessant promotion of the vulgarity of pop culture has "elevated trash to the status of great art, while genuinely great Western art is treated as trash."

School and college curriculums have been totally rewritten, producing a generation of academic and moral illiterates. This new (supposedly improved) form of education has obliterated our American heritage and everything for which this country has stood. What is now considered to be "the good life" has been distorted beyond recognition.[6] Rock music, the celebration of drugs, and the demand for sexual liberation were the three inseparable monuments of the revolution. Boundless freedom was promised, but moral chaos and the coarsening of feeling and sensibility have been the result.

As with most revolutions, the call for total freedom became a demand for total control:

> *The phenomenon of political correctness, with its speech codes and other efforts to enforce ideological conformity, was one the predictable result of this transformation which began at the University of California at Berkeley with the Free Speech Movement ... [which] soon degenerated into an effort to abridge freedom by dictating what could and could not be said about any number of politically sensitive issues.*[7]

While the slogan was "free speech," this was not the real issue; students already had that. What they were really demanding was that universities give over their facilities for radical political action, without restriction. Their demand for "free speech" was nothing less than a demand that universities change from academic institutions into a coordinated, effective operating base for political radicalism.[8]

The structure, order, traditions and morals of Western civilization stood in their way. Consider the spectacle of hordes of demonstrating college students mindlessly chanting "Hi-ho, Hi-ho Western Civ has to go."

They got what they demanded. Academic standards were destroyed, curriculums dumbed down, and politics brought into the very heart of the educational process.[9] Faculty hiring and promotion, decisions concerning curriculums, grading, methods of teaching, and student life were all politicized. The idea that preference should be based on achievement, and that everyone is equal before the law (liberal or conservative) were shamelessly abandoned in the face of political pressure. Everything became political.[10]

There was very little the radicals demanded they did not get, Afro-American study programs, women's studies, gay studies, gender and transgender studies, as well as race-segregated classrooms and dormitories. Racial, religious and sexual discrimination were all institutionalized as liberal virtues under the banner of "affirmative action," supposedly ending the injustice of discrimination by mandating further acts of discrimination

College administrators all over the country caved in to the militant demands of the radical students. The cave-in at Cornell University in April 1969 is a graphic illustration of what was happening across the nation.

What Happened At Cornell

Cornell president James A. Perkins instituted a program in the mid-1960s to recruit black students whose SAT scores were well below the average of Cornell's entering class. As a result, black student enrollment rose from 25 to about 250. Seeking solidarity, they banded together and formed an Afro-American Society and began making demands for separate black-only living quarters, black-only Afro-American studies programs, and a degree-granting college within the college for the exclusive use of black students in order to "create the tools necessary for the formation of a black nation." Incredibly, Perkins agreed.[11]

This was followed by an escalating pattern of non-negotiable demands, vandalism, and violence. Buildings were occupied, hostages taken, and college property destroyed. Finally, in the spring of 1969 during parent's weekend, some one hundred black students armed with knives, rifles and ammunition belts, forcibly ejected approximately thirty parents and forty college employees from a meeting hall, while college officials did nothing. A thirty-five-hour occupation of the building followed. The students said they were protesting because of Cornell's "racist attitudes" and because it "lacked a program relevant to black students."

One of their demands was that disciplinary action against three black students involved in an earlier incident be dropped. The vice president of public affairs promised to recommend to the faculty that they vote to nullify the reprimands. An agreement was reached, and the black students triumphantly vacated the building, clutching their rifles and ammunition belts with clenched fists raised in defiance.

A divided Cornell faculty then met and voted to *not* dismiss the penalties by 726 to 281. In a furious response, some 2,500 white and black radical students, many carrying guns, demanded a reversal in the faculty vote, declaring that "Cornell has three hours to live . . . we are moving tonight." A thoroughly frightened and intimidated faculty met again and caved in to the rioters' demands. The majority agreed with a philosophy professor who assured the rioters "we want to be your friends." [12]

Further humiliations followed. That evening, when President Perkins went to address the students, he was publicly mocked by a black student who kept him waiting to speak. Then a white student grabbed a soft drink can from Perkins' hand, lifted it for all to see, drank from it and handed it back to the president. When Perkins was finally allowed to speak, he saluted the meeting as "one of the most positive forces ever set in motion in the history of Cornell." [13]

THE AFTERMATH

Perkins' capitulation (and others like it) to the totalitarian demands of the student radicals had far-reaching ramifications. Political philosopher Walter Berns, a professor at Cornell in the 1960s, noted that:

> *By surrendering to students armed with guns, Perkins had made it easier for those who came after him to surrender to students armed only with epithets (racists, sexists, elitists, homophobes); By inaugurating a black studies program, Perkins paved the way for Latino studies programs, women's studies programs, and multi cultural studies programs; by failing to support a professor's freedom to teach, he paved the way for speech codes and political correctness; and, of course, he pioneered the practice of affirmative action admissions and hiring.* [14]

The deep-rooted and, to date, unchangeable results of America's Cultural Revolution were scarcely imaginable forty-five years ago. Furthermore, conservatives have been virtually ineffective in their efforts to restore any kind of sane, moral order to our society. As author Kimball observes:

> *The long march of America's Cultural Revolution has succeeded beyond the wildest dreams of all but the most starry-eyed utopians. The great irony is that this victory took place in the midst of a significant drift to the center-right in electoral politics. The startling and depressing fact is that supposedly conservative victories at the polls have done absolutely nothing to challenge the dominance of left-wing, emancipationist attitudes and ideas in our culture . . . [I]n the so-called "cultural wars," conservatives have been conspicuous as losers.* [15]

The Cultural Revolution of the 1960s and 70s profoundly changed the nature of America. Supreme Court rulings removed prayer and Bible reading from public schools and began removing anything Christian from government or state-owned buildings. When God was thrown out, we sharply turned the corner to becoming a godless, humanist society. The education system, the news and entertainment media, the political process and politicians themselves all began turning that corner. Public morality turned the corner. What was once considered immoral became acceptable and was elevated, even celebrated, while what was once considered godly, right and proper was ridiculed and cast aside. Traditional family values, and indeed the nature and stability of the family itself—which is the fundamental building block of society—also turned the corner and plunged. Crime rates soared, particularly among teenagers and young people, as did the divorce rate, unwed pregnancies and other measures of the moral state of society. And the church was in no state to combat these changes, as their moral statistics were virtually no different than those of the rest of society. We became a totally different people. America has become a totally different place.

CHAPTER 11

PULLING IT ALL TOGETHER

We need to summarize where the betrayal of our nation over the past 85 years has finally brought us, and what the future now looks like. Two questions will come to mind that are tremendously significant. Given the great beginning and development of our nation, why have all these things come upon us—America of all places! What happened? And then, how can we face the future with hope? To address these questions, we must know something of America's forgotten, re-written history. This is absolutely essential to making any kind of sense out of what is happening, and why. But first, we will look at the nature and cost of *liberty*. After all, its loss is what our present state is about!

THE NATURE OF LIBERTY AND WHAT IT HAS COST

Americans have traditionally believed that man was born to be free—free to run his own life before God according to His moral law and the dictates of conscience. Liberty is then intuitively seen as a state in which man was intended to live. To be robbed of liberty is unnatural to our design and purpose. When this happens in a society, it will be in a perpetual state of unrest and strife—never at peace within itself. Liberty is a delicate and fragile thing, and if we take it for granted, and don't guard and fight to protect it, it will be easily stolen from us. And liberty is more than just something worth defending—*it is priceless!* It is worth fighting for, worth dying to maintain or recover for its own sake, for our sake, and for the sake of our progeny and all future generations.

America's founders differentiated between freedom and liberty. You can't have liberty without first having freedom. Freedom will then become license to do whatever you want, or it can be transformed into liberty. They thought of liberty as *freedom under the constraint of God's moral law*. For example, I may be free (able) to take something you have that I want; but *I am not at liberty to do so*, because God's law constrains me. "Thou shalt not steal." In a fallen world in which selfishness prevails, we can't be allowed to do anything we want. The rights of others have to be respected, which comes through observing a just system of law. It is the biblical role of civil government to provide and enact such law.

When liberty is increasingly curtailed, it invariably leads to totalitarian government and oppressive law. On the other hand, the absence or breakdown of government and law results in anarchy. Both are disastrous to society. In our fallen world, *liberty and government need each other.* A delicate balance between these polar opposites is essential for a peaceful, prosperous society. When they are out of balance, liberty and government become enemies. It can be persuasively argued that America, as it was founded, is the closest any nation has come to achieving that balance. As such, America became "the land of liberty" to millions who migrated to our shores. It became a beacon of hope to others in the world who looked for us to stand strong in the defense of liberty against expanding totalitarianism in any way that we could.

From where did our liberty come? It did not just happen. Before the first settlers came to this land, it had to be wrest by sacrifice and blood from the same breed of tyrants and dictators we see today who want to control our property, our lives, and how we think. The liberty we have so mindlessly enjoyed did not come free. Just look at history! The story of blood-bought spiritual and religious liberty goes back to the Reformation, when brave, spirited men and women were burned at the stake and died from other forms of diabolical torture for their faith. They refused to deny their Lord and God and be told what to believe. To save their lives and buy a few extra years of miserable earthly existence in forced conformity to a false, totalitarian form of faith was simply unthinkable to them.

Freedom from tyranny eventually comes when people of unshakable spiritual and religious convictions are willing to stand and die for them. Freedom to worship God according to their Christian conscience was to them more precious than life itself. The martyrs of the Reformation inspired and motivated Christians that came after them to suffer or fight for the sake of freedom—or flee to where they could live in Christian liberty.

Thus, America was born!

They came so they could live in liberty of conscience according to their religious and political beliefs and convictions. Living in that liberty is what America is all about. James Madison, considered the father of America's Constitution and its Bill of Rights, once said that "conscience is the most sacred of all property."

America's Founding Fathers warned us that the price of maintaining our liberty is eternal vigilance. However, we have not been vigilant. We became complacent, and we are now fast losing our liberty. As this happens, we return to the oppressive form of government and state of society from which our forefathers fled to establish this great country. Shame on us for our lack of vigilance—just look at what it has come to today!

The last one hundred years has seen a return of the same spirit of hateful intolerance and brutality in our world that motivated and empowered religious totalitarians of the Reformation era. *The 20th century saw more Christians killed and martyred for their faith than in all the preceding centuries since Christ combined!*[1] Countless thousands have rotted in prison, or died in concentration camps because they refused to cave in to their captors and deny their faith and their God. And the 21st century promises to be even worse as more and more Christians are tortured, beheaded, and crucified because of their faith.

History has shown that whenever Christians come under intense persecution, two things happen. First, *the church is purged and purified.* All those who have been playing church, acting out a "religion," simply drop out—the cost is too high. Only those who personally know and experience the presence of the Living God remain. *Then, the church grows.* And *the more it is persecuted, the more it grows!* Why is that? What do people see in persecuted Christians that draws them to their God, and come under the same persecution?

The answer can first be seen in the Roman Coliseum and other such places in the early years of Christendom. The public flocked to see Christians being torn apart by wild animals and hacked to pieces for their "entertainment." And the totally unexpected result was that thousands of spectators became Christians! What they saw stirred something deep within. They saw Christians lovingly comforting one another, praying, and praising God even as they were facing death, and when they were being brutally killed. They were not shaking their fists in hate at the watching authorities, as they would have done in their place.

To those who were open, what they saw transcended all evil and hate, and from their innermost being they knew this was an expression of a love—a Truth—that is higher and better than anything they had ever experienced or seen! They knew this was how they ought to live their lives—but didn't (and couldn't). Something from within cried out at what they saw, "These Christians have something I want with all my being. I don't care what it costs, I must have it!" They were compelled from within to seek out those early Christians and join them. And so it was that under intense persecution, the early church grew like wild-fire. It has been the same down through the ages, right up to now.

In today's skeptical world, "religion" is considered a refuge for the ignorant and weak-minded. Is that what we see demonstrated here? Can the world explain Christian martyrdom as coming from weakness; can it be explained in terms of Maslow's hierarchy of needs? I think not! Man's inner-most need has been described as "a God shaped vacuum in the heart of every man which cannot be filled by any created thing, but only by God, the Creator, made known through Jesus." [2]

The liberty that we now so thoughtlessly enjoy was bought by those who in past times found this God, this Jesus, and lived this faith—and were willing to die for it. He can still be found by those who diligently seek Him!

FROM WHERE HAVE WE COME? AMERICA'S FOUNDING CULTURE

The present plight of our society and nation can only be seen in proper perspective when we know something about our beginning. We need to know what kind of people founded this nation, why they came here and how they governed themselves. Until we know something of this, we will not fully comprehend the tragedy of our present state (or perhaps even know that we *are* in any sort of tragic state). When we understand from where we have come, we can clearly see how far we have fallen. The more clearly we see this, the more deeply we are motivated to cry out to God for mercy and deliverance, and offer ourselves to be used of Him in answering our cry.

Just Who Were The Early American Colonists?

Five great waves of immigrants came to the shores of North America between 1620 and 1775, and most of them came for basically the same reason—to escape from some form of persecution and live in liberty.

The first to come and establish a settlement of families were the Pilgrims. We shall look briefly at just a little of their story because it reveals so much about the nature and character of the people who laid the foundation of this nation. They had discovered from a diligent study of the Scriptures the way of salvation and the biblical principles by which they were to live. They were a well educated group (three of them were graduates of Cambridge University, very rare in those days) and they saw little resemblance between the early New Testament church and the mandatory state-run Church of England. Believing the church was beyond reform, they illegally separated themselves from it, and as "non-conformists" came under dogged, even intense persecution from the state.

They left their native England under great duress, and eventually immigrated to America, arriving on the *Mayflower* in November, 1620. Because of delays it was far later in the year than they had planned, and they were much further north. They had to build their shelters in bitterly cold weather, for which they were totally unprepared. Terrible sickness set in, and in the first two months, almost half their number died. Of the 16 mothers of families in their company, only 4 survived. Of the twenty-five fathers of families (some had left their wives in Holland), only 12 survived. [3] And yet, when the *Mayflower* returned to England in the spring, *not one of the Pilgrims went back with it!* They knew with all their being that God had called them to this. One text was burned into their hearts; "No one, after putting his hand to the plow and looking back, is fit for the kingdom of God." [4]

The Pilgrims not only brought and established religious and political liberty to this land, they also established economic liberty. The English merchant company that had financed their expedition had insisted that they establish a communal system of living. It was thought that this would maximize their chance of survival in their new hostile environment, and therefore more likely to pay back their loan (which they did, in full). Under this system, the land they settled was to be communally owned and their crops shared equally. However, after two years of near starvation, Governor Bradford had to abandon the system and allot private land to families and individuals, who were then responsible to feed themselves from what they produced. At the following harvest, without any increase in the land under cultivation, food production was tripled! They never went hungry again. The Pilgrims thus established that their material needs were best met through private ownership, individual incentive and voluntary exchange (aka Capitalism).

The Puritans came shortly after the Pilgrims. They had tried to purify the Church of England from within, and were so persecuted for their efforts that they began coming to America in 1630. Of all the early settlers, they have been the most misrepresented and maligned. They were first called "Puritans" because of their trying to purify the state church, but also because of their desire to live pure lives before God. They believed strongly in the reformation of society in every realm—education, politics, economics, medicine and science. The universities of Harvard and Yale were founded by Puritans in the 1630s as centers of Christian education in all disciplines. A far cry from what they have become!

Next came a wave of Anglican immigrants, who came because of the rise to political power of the Presbyterians following the English Civil War. Then came the Quakers, who were persecuted simply because they were different. Finally, the Scottish Presbyterians, who came in large numbers because of their persecution after the 1707 union of England and Scotland, when mandatory membership in the Church of England was being forced upon them.

These were the people who founded America. By the time of the War of Independence, the population of the thirteen colonies consisted mainly of those who had migrated here in order to escape some form of persecution and live in liberty and their descendants.

America's Early Christian Culture And Self-Government

The early colonists held strong biblical beliefs under the assumption that men are responsible beings, capable of ordering their own affairs for which they are accountable to God (not the state). This was exemplified in America's founding society and government, where the fundamental belief in man's ability and accountability minimized the role of civil government in people's lives and maximized individual liberty. Early American writers called this form of inner government *Christian self-government*, meaning the exercise of man's free will in voluntarily submitting to the internal government of their life according to Christ and the Christian scriptures.

This principle of internal Christian government was also applied to the civil government of each local community. It was simply referred to as *Local self-government*. By this, every town and village in colonial America governed their own affairs according to their shared religious beliefs and convictions, with little or no dependence on outside management or money. Government was never spoken of as *them*, but always in terms of *us*. The work of government was done *by* them, not *for* them. It was carried out in the full light of public scrutiny, in which they tested their own decisions and corrected their own errors. It was highly successful because it developed a deep sense of personal and civic responsibility. They knew in what they believed and were committed to living it out in their personal and corporate lives. It developed the uniquely American concept of *Liberty*.[5]

Where necessary, this system of local self-government was extended to the formation of county governments, which had the responsibility for such things as a central courthouse to serve a group of townships (each town being too small to warrant its own courthouse). The authority of county governments was derived from their constituent townships, and was limited to the specific responsibilities delegated to them by those townships. And a colonial government handled their relation to the other colonies and the rest of the world, which were their limited realm of responsibility.

Each level of civil government had no more responsibility and authority than was needed to operate within its designated level. The fundamental and residual political power remained at the lowest possible level—the individual citizens within each local community. The whole system was in every way a bottom up form of government.

America Was Shaped By Spiritual Awakenings

America has been shaped by two great spiritual awakenings. The first (c.1730- 40) produced the principles of liberty—and the men who so passionately expounded them—that became the basis of the eventual fight for Independence and the foundation of America's government. *There would not be an independent United States of America as it came to be, "Land of the free and home of the brave," had there not been that First Great Spiritual Awakening!*

America's Second Great Awakening came in the early to mid-1800s and gave America a social conscience and compassionate heart. A great network of benevolent Christian societies and movements was born that ministered to the physical, social, *as well as* the spiritual needs of people at home and abroad. America became the missionary center of the world, with by far the highest per-capita giving for humanitarian aid in the world. Anywhere there was a natural disaster, famine, or great need in the world, America was there—as a government *and* as private, individual donors.

And this great awakening finally awakened the conscience of the nation into that epic, tragic but necessary struggle to put an end to slavery. A struggle in which over six hundred thousand white Americans died, giving 4 million slaves their freedom. Every civilization in history has had slavery, but America is the only nation that has had a civil war to free its slaves, a war in which the slaves themselves were not one of the combatant sides!

America Became A Great Nation Under Christianity And Capitalism

America became the beacon of liberty and hope throughout the world, and people started coming here en-mass to live. Some forty million Europeans migrated to America in the eighteenth and nineteenth centuries. And they are still pouring in! They came in such numbers because this land offered two things that men everywhere want—*Freedom* and *Prosperity*. They came because America honored God and His Law, *and God will honor those who honor Him!* They came because of its foundational biblical belief that government should keep out of people's everyday lives, enabling them to live in personal, religious, economic, and political liberty.

They came to America because its free market economy produced unimagined wealth. Capitalism produces economic inequality in a way that *ensures economic justice.* Some people are smarter or work harder than others, and are rewarded accordingly. That is how it should be—*it is just!* Justice is *not* satisfied by equalizing personal wealth. It is satisfied by ensuring that people can keep and control the fruit of their own honest labor.

Furthermore—since Capitalism is so maligned today and widely considered to be a "bad" system—we should know that Capitalism is a *reflector* of values, not a generator of values! As such, it is *amoral*. It will provide whatever product or service society wants. If Capitalism provides what is "bad," it is because society has bad values—*not because capitalism is a bad system!* On the other hand, Socialism *generates and promotes* values which are centered on the power, authority and importance of the state. Under this system, the personal wealth of some is plundered by force of law and redistributed to others in the name of "economic equality" and so-called "social justice." It is a great vote-winner, since far more people are recipients of this wealth than those being plundered! By this process, everyone is supposed to "get their fair share." Under this totalitarian control of society's wealth, some unjustly lose while others unjustly gain. *Injustice prevails on every hand!*

It should be noted that a free-market economy is assumed throughout the Scriptures in that *everyone* has the right to own and control private property. This is enshrined in the commandment "Thou shalt not steal," which applies to *everyone* (including government). The biblical function of civil government is very specific—it is to *protect* our God-given rights (which includes life, liberty and property). This primary purpose is recognized in the American Declaration of Independence immediately following its enumeration of God-given rights, "That to secure these rights, governments are instituted among men, deriving their just powers from the consent of the governed."

And the "just powers" of government means its power is to be exercised in strict, impartial justice, showing favor to no one. This is also thoroughly biblical, and can be seen, for example, in the command to the nation's leaders, "You shall do no injustice in judgment; you shall not be partial to the poor nor defer to the great, but you are to judge your neighbor fairly."[6] This injunction specifically prohibits government welfare programs, which very specifically favors the poor. This does not mean that God doesn't care about the poor and needy, but simply it is not the job of government to provide for them.

The Bible clearly put this responsibility upon individuals, not their government. "Now when you reap the harvest of your land, you shall not reap to the very corners of your field, nor shall you gather the gleanings of your harvest . . . you shall leave them for the needy and for the stranger. I am the LORD your God."[7] It should be noted that the poor and needy were not given direct handouts. Food was to be left for them, but they had to come and gather it for themselves!

The Change In America's Founding Legal System And Its Effect

All law is based on a system of morals that define right and wrong, which must come from a "religious" base. All religions in some way address the basic questions and issues of life and the values by which it should be lived, which may or may not include God. This was recognized in a Supreme Court opinion which called Secular Humanism a religion without a God. [8] *All* law is legalized morality—whatever the source of that morality might be. To say that you cannot legislate morality is plainly absurd. The issue is not whether or not morality can be legislated, it is *whose, or what morality* will be used for the basis of law. The two fundamental options are the base provided by God's Law, or that provided by man-conceived humanistic ideals. [9]

It can then be seen that law is inextricably tied to its "theological" base, meaning its belief or non-belief concerning God and all associated moral values. And if the theological base of a nation's legal system is changed, the entire nation will eventually be changed, including its system of education, its economy, its policies, and certainly the nature of family life. This happened in America in the late nineteenth and early twentieth centuries, which opened the door for all the changes that have flooded our nation since then.

America's early legal system was based on William Blackstone (1723–80), English jurist and writer. His *Commentaries on the Laws of England* (1765), was based on the teachings of Scripture. He believed;

> – Man is subject to the will of His Maker, referred to as *"the Laws of Nature and of Nature's God"* (a phrase found in the Declaration of Independence, which directly reflected Blackstone's ideas and teachings).
> – God provided the only valid foundation for all law. *"No human law should be suffered to contradict these."*
> – The scope of God's Law is universal, applicable to *"It is binding over all the globe in all countries, and at all times."*
> – And any man-made law that violates God's law is not a valid law.

Blackstone's teachings were the basis of all legal education, legal decisions and legal counsel in America. Because the legal system was based on Scripture, law students had to spend the first year of their education studying theology, right alongside those who were studying for the ministry. The Bible was considered to be the only valid basis for law, and was so respected, that for many years it was the only book allowed in the jury room. Under this biblically-based legal system, America experienced stability of the family; marriage a covenant relationship and divorce almost completely unknown; the lowest crime rate of any nation; the highest morality of any nation; great material prosperity from the flourishing free market economy; and the highest literacy rate in the world.

The decline of America and the turning from its roots goes back to when the theological base of our legal system was changed. In 1870, C.C. Langdell became dean of the Harvard Law School (the nation's leading law school) and he began to change the foundation of America's legal system. He was a disciple of Charles Darwin and did not accept Blackstone's *Commentaries.* He believed that law should be based on man's experience, on current, dominant social values and interests. Roscoe Pound, Harvard Law School dean 1916 to 1936, a disciple of Langdell, described this new bases for law as "sociological jurisprudence." He executed the changeover by systematically and deliberately removing God from the legal system, replacing Him with the state. The completed change was announced in a 1926 lecture by Pound in which he said, "Thus, the cycle is complete; we are back to the State as the unchangeable authority behind legal precepts. The State takes the place of Jehovah." [10]

This literally changed the theological base of our whole legal system! Jehovah was thrown out and "the State" became god. America was thus returned to the same legal and governmental base of the nations from which our early settlers had fled to live in liberty. *Yes, the cycle had indeed been completed. We went all the way back to square-one!* Pound accurately and approvingly predicted that this change would result in limitations on the use of private property; liability without fault (giving rise to no-fault divorce and no-fault insurance); social interests taking precedence over individual interests; and parental rights being subservient to what the state determines those rights should be. And this was just the very tip of the iceberg of what was to come. And this is a *better* legal system?

SO WHAT DO WE NOW FACE?

Gramsci's long march is coming to the end of its mission, as there is not much left of the moral standards and beliefs by which we once lived. Our society is relentlessly moving toward the inexorable climax of its total transformation and destruction. We have been betrayed and manipulated to the point where our great republic, and everything for which America has stood, is about to be irrevocably lost.

The impending collapse of our economy will be devastating and bring America to its knees. Chaos will result and martial law will be implemented. What is left of our Constitution will be discarded, and totalitarian government will take control of virtually every aspect of life. Our liberties and rights as free

Americans will be lost. Bible-believing Christians are being increasingly defined as a hate group and source of "right wing terrorism." They will soon come under great persecution to rid society of their "hateful" beliefs and practices.

The Cold War, the titanic struggle between the West and Marxist globalism we all thought was dead will soon become a very "hot" war. Russia is actively preparing for war with America to become the world's number one superpower.[11] They have rebuilt their military, and according to official numbers, they are strategically on a par with America. However, the numbers assume that Russian has not cheated in the arms-control game, which ignores the nature of their leadership and their history of violating every treaty we have made with them. A former Soviet analyst at the CIA and the Defense Intelligence Agency, William F. Lee, claims in his book, *The ABM Treaty Charade* that Russia has a vast hidden stockpile of ICBMs that was never accounted for after the fall of the Soviet Union.[12] And the comparative nuclear warhead count ignores the fact that Russian missiles have almost three times the destructive effect of our own, which, as we have seen, is extremely significant in taking out hardened military targets. Russia has hardened their key military facilities and weapons to a far greater degree than we have.

Russia has developed new generations of strategic nuclear missiles significantly more advanced than our own, and against which America presently has no defense. America's primary strategic weapons (ICBMs, SLBMs, cruise missiles) are left-overs from the Cold War era, based on 25-40 year-old technology. Russia has also developed more advanced cruise missiles, and long range surface-to-air missiles than ours—the S-300 and S-400. They are considered to be the best in the world, very difficult for even our most advanced aircraft to penetrate; and Russia will start deploying the even more advanced S-500 system in 2016.

As well as their huge military build-up, Russia is now preparing their population for eventual war. They have an on-going public-media anti-America propaganda campaign, strongly blaming us for their economic woes and accusing us of trying to encircle them and threaten their country. The campaign is having effect, as anti-American sentiment in Russia is said to be greater now than it was during the Cold War.[13] The American government has been oblivious to what Russia is doing until fairly recently (after all, we won the Cold War—right?), but we are now belatedly starting to take serious notice.

China is also rapidly building their military with, among other things, the capacity to take out an American carrier task force in defense of their territorial waters. They fully intend to take back Taiwan and expand their borders in other areas as well, but America, which has a defense pact with Taiwan, stands in their way. China's expansion is an essential part of their long-term plans, so for some time they have been planning for eventual war with America. [14] While we have not taken this very seriously (just look at all the trade China would lose), our government is only now taking steps to prepare for the possibility. [15]

All this gets very little coverage in America's news media, even though it has often come up in Congressional hearings and concerned comments by military leaders. Congress was just recently told (March 2016) by two senior Pentagon generals that Russia and China are developing the capacity to knock out our essential military satellite communications in a future war. [16] If successful, our capacity to fight would be crippled. (The imminent possibility of massive conflict is well discussed and presented in the book *The New Tactics of Global War – Reflections on the Changing Balance of Power in the Final Days of Peace* by Benjamin Baruch and J.R. Nyquist. 2015.)

In summary, America is facing very real threats from two major groups. First, the nuclear powered Marxist states of Russia and China, who are presently in close league with each other. (North Korea could be considered a viable wild-card Marxist threat of its own.) The second group consists of various Muslim nations and allied terrorist groups led by Iran, which is about to become a nuclear power, whose weapons could be used directly against us, or through their proxy terrorist groups.

America is standing in the way of the global ambitions of all these groups. The nuclear weapons we face are controlled by secular or religious psychopaths. Unless there is a fundamental change in the way evil-minded people think and act (that is, a change in basic human nature), or an act of Providence intervenes, some of these weapons *will* be used against America, and will involve some form of invasion and fighting on our own soil. Large, well organized terrorist groups have already infiltrated American soil through our virtually wide-open borders, and they continue to enter. At the right time, they will burst upon us.

And what is America doing by way of response? [17] We reduce the size of our nuclear forces, as well as drastically cut back our Army, Navy and Air Force. The Army recently announced a forty thousand troop reduction by 2017, bringing it to its lowest level since before WW II. [18] In 2016, the Air Force budget is being "drastically cut" [19] and the Navy is absorbing a $7 billion budget cut. And of course we talk and negotiate a lot, our leaders considering themselves to be experts in the art. As in the old Cold War days, our leaders still have far more confidence in the "tongue" than the "sword!" We act nice and accommodating to countries on the above list, even signing agreements that give them the store.

America is being openly prepared from within to be taken down and have its sovereignty as a free, independent nation removed so it can be brought under global government control. What will it take for the American people to wake up? When will we begin to call our leaders to account for their *high treason against our beloved nation?!*

WHY HAS ALL THIS HAPPENED TO AMERICA?

Our brief review of America's founding history (not the re-written version) reveals the godly nature of our heritage. We were once a people who called upon God and put our trust in Him. God's ways and laws were foundational to early America. We honored God, and He honored and blessed us. This placed upon our shoulders a great responsibility and degree of accountability to diligently preserve our blessings and all we have been given. The Scriptures tell us "And from everyone who has been given much shall much be required." [20]

As we see how America prospered, and was blessed to become the leader of the free world, and we compare that to the immoral state of our society and the deception, betrayal and corruption of our leadership, we should be horrified at the failure of God's people—and indeed our whole should-have-known-better society at large—in allowing all this to happen. It could have been stopped. All we had to do was wake up, kick out those who were obviously stealing our liberty, corrupting our government and destroying our nation, and replace them with those who understood what it historically means to be American. *But we didn't.* We should know that our present state is a tragic example of what has been called *The Natural Law of Consequences,* a fundamental biblical principle that is found throughout the Scriptures. A well known example states; "whatever a man sows, this he will also reap." [21]

Choices, *be they personal or national,* have consequences!

To apply this principle more specifically to America: There is a direct relationship between our blindly standing by and allowing our nation to be taken over by the godless and systematically transformed into a godless state (*which is what we have sown*); and the present disastrous state of our economy, our government and our whole society (*which is what we now reap*).

The administration and leadership we now have are exactly what we deserve. Some may say they have been *allowed* to naturally rise to the top, like dross in a boiling caldron, but I believe God is more directly involved than that in who leads a nation in which He has been so directly involved and has so richly blessed. In other words, our present leaders can be seen as God's men for the hour, not because He approves of who they are or what they do, but because God is using them to bring consequential judgment upon a nation that has turned its back upon Him. In the same way the Babylonian king Nebuchadnezzar was once God's man for the hour in bringing consequential judgment upon the rebellious nation of Judah. God specifically appointed him and set him up for this purpose. God did not *generate* the evil of the Babylonians, He used what was already there for the purpose of judgment, and later punished them severely for their wickedness, as He will in today's situation.

God's primary purpose in judgment has not been to "do us in" or destroy us, but to *awaken* God's people and call us back to Himself so He can restore us. He has been waiting for the cry of our response. If it does not come, then the full force of His judgment will come.

As a nation, we will eventually cry out to Him!

Let us look briefly at this from a broad historical perspective. In Old Testament times, Israel was founded by God, and became a nation of God's people. They were raised, blessed, and called to be a nation of priests through whom all the world would be blessed. When they turned their back on Him and followed the false gods and ways of surrounding nations, He repeatedly warned them through His prophets, calling them back to Himself. When they continued to ignore Him, in their *spiritual* blindness God gave them over to *intellectual* blindness. (There is a natural correlation!) They became as fools, making stupid decisions, as God Himself stated, "For My people are foolish, they know Me not; they are stupid children and have no understanding. They are shrewd to do evil, but to do good they do not know."[22]

When the natural consequences of their foolishness did not awaken them, God finally brought judgment. He unleashed upon them a people who were biblically described as the most ferocious, ruthless people of that time, people without mercy who would kill just for the sake of killing. First, the Assyrians, who utterly destroyed and disbursed the ten northern tribes of Israel (722 BC). Then later, over a period of some twenty years (606 BC to 586 BC), the Babylonians overcame the southern kingdom of Judah, took them captive to Babylon for seventy years and totally destroyed Jerusalem.

Now fast forward to New Testament times and re-cap for a moment. God was deeply involved in the establishment of the United States of America. As a nation of His people, He blessed us, bringing us to worldwide prominence to be the most prosperous and freest of all nations, and the missionary center of the world. **Do we honestly suppose we can turn our back on all that, go our own way and serve the gods of our modern age and get no response from God?**

As in Old Testament times, in our spiritual blindness God has given us over to intellectual and just plain common sense blindness. We have become absolute fools, incapable of seeing the obvious in what is happening all around us, even the most common-sense-obvious, because we have refused to acknowledge the spiritually obvious. Perhaps it is no accident that the most ferocious, cruel and ruthless people on the planet today, who show no mercy and will kill just for the sake of killing, are turned against America and are totally dedicated to bringing us down. And incidentally, they happen to come from the same national territories that God used to discipline Israel and Judah over 2500 years ago.

WHERE HAS THE CHURCH BEEN?

Where has the church been throughout all this turmoil and change? What effect has it had? It is supposed to be a watchdog and guide to the course that society is taking. That was certainly true in early America, where it was key to guiding the course of our nation. Colonialists of the eighteenth and early nineteenth centuries were the most enlightened and educated people of their time. From their writings, their newspapers, and their private correspondence and public speeches, it can be seen that they understood the principles of civil government and their relation to liberty. They understood the meaning of liberty in its four basic forms—personal, religious, economic, and political. They understood the biblical source and foundation of these liberties and how they were to be protected by civil government. They were well aware of the teachings and application of Scripture in these areas, and their responsibilities as Christian citizens.

All this learning and understanding emanated from America's pulpits and the writings of ministers. The oppression and tyranny of the English government over the American colonists and the denial of their fundamental rights as Englishmen had led ministers to seek to understand the source and nature of their rights and liberties, and to know how they should respond biblically to the increasing tyranny under which they lived. They were at the forefront of this search for this truth. They read Locke, Grotius, Sidney, Montesquieu, Blackstone, Smith, and other contemporary and recent writers, who had started to question the nature of liberty and the basis of civic responsibility and social order. Their writings were measured against the Scriptures, and in the process, ministers were awakened to the meaning, application and responsibilities of Christian liberty and the biblical role of civil government. This can be attested to by the many sermons that have come down from that era.[23] Most sermons then were written, read from the pulpit, and then published for the congregation to study and check out for themselves, which they did!

So what happened? Where is the church today?

The most revealing indicator of the state of the American church at large today is the simple fact that with regards to the culture and the way society is now operated, it has been virtually powerless! Scripture asserts that the Kingdom of God does not consist of words, but of power. But America now operates in a moral and spiritual vacuum. The once respected and influential church has effectively been shut out and no longer sets the moral tone and standards of society. The education establishment and the popular media now do that very effectively from an openly anti-Christian base. Lost is America's historically held general belief that a prevailing respect and observance of God's moral standards is the essential basis for *both* personal and civil liberty.

Christianity and biblical principles no longer have any say in the determination of domestic or foreign policy, or in any serious public debate on these issues. Christianity is considered to be irrelevant, and symbols of its once foundational presence are systematically removed from the public square. And in general, today's church does not seem too bothered by it! Church life goes on as usual, pretty much unmoved by what is happening "out there." While some certainly are trying to turn our nation around, or at least stem the tide, it has to be admitted that little is achieved. The state of society and our whole nation continues to deteriorate.

Would it then be too much to suggest that if the church has been powerless to halt the removal of Christian morality from this once-Christian society— powerless to halt the plunge of our nation into spiritual bankruptcy—that the church itself has become spiritually bankrupt? And perhaps that is small wonder, as most professing Christians today seem to have little interest or desire to "pursue holiness" and walk by the Spirit in the ways of God. Their Christianity is all about *them*! There is little interest in truly knowing God, experiencing what He is really like, and seeking to bring joy to His heart. All that matters is to be "saved."

Compare this to what the church and our society was like during the Second Great Awakening of the early to mid nineteenth century. Compare it to what it means to be a Christian in the Middle East today, where countless Muslims are coming to Jesus Christ, totally sold out to Him.[24] Over there and in other parts of the world, Christians are being cruelly tortured and are dying for their faith. God has no Rapture for them! Only in America has the church embraced self-serving doctrines that allow them to continue in sin and then be whisked out of harm's way when real persecution comes. We are the modern-day "Leodicean" church, and before God brings final judgment upon America, His church is going to be persecuted and purged. It is coming soon!

Another revealing indicator of the state of the church is that America has not seen widespread society-transforming revival for over one hundred and sixty years. There have been times of God's moving, but little effect on society itself. Although the "Jesus movement" of the early 1970s saw many genuinely came to Him, the deterioration of our culture actually accelerated during that decade.

There has been nothing like the great awakenings of our past that had a profound effect on society and the course our nation took. The church should be crying out *"Why?"* But it is not. The modern church at large has no serious interest in revival, with little or no understanding of what a genuine revival is, or how desperately they need to be revived in another great national spiritual awakening.

Christians should be shocked and appalled at the immoral, corrupt, ungodly state of our nation. We should be on our knees, crying out to God and desperately asking *where is God, where is the power of the church to bring back a godless society, what has happened to us!?* But most have turned a blind eye, as if they had no historical or present part in our nation's precipitous decline. The church has no idea how awesomely accountable we are for the state of our nation. *God will ultimately hold Christians primarily accountable for the state of America's society— not those who are systematically destroying it!* The church (as a body of believers, not as organizational entities) will have to answer to God for why we are no longer a Christian nation, and for the trashing of our Christian culture!

The church is key to America's past, present and whatever future we have as a nation. It was an inseparable part of the founding of our nation; it has a high level of accountability for the disastrous decline of our nation; and if awakened before it is too late, it will be inseparably tied to the (hopeful) restoration of our nation.

Of the major worldviews, three of them expect or demand from their followers total sacrificial dedication to their cause and a willingness to die for it. They are Islam, Marxism/Communism, and biblical Christianity. And now the first two are dedicated to wiping out the third one. Church, it's time to wake up and get on our knees! *This is truly the "Battle of the Ages!"*

WHEREIN LIES OUR HOPE

Given the messed-up, corrupt state of our society and government, its failing economy and our geopolitical vulnerability, what hope can we have for our nation? We are in the midst of God's well-deserved judgment and we cannot expect that He will simply set it all aside, no matter how hard we pray or what we do. However, God was providentially involved in the foundation of our nation, and we can still hope for some level of reprieve from the full judgment that is about to come upon us if we cry out to him in faith and true repentance. To put it simply, this is where our hope now lies!

We must understand that nothing will be accomplished by simply over-hauling the political process, or replacing our politicians, no matter how good they might be. It is the *heart* of our nation that has to be changed, which is a spiritual, not a political issue. This is not to say that Christians should not be politically involved in doing what we can at that level as God leads us, but our hope cannot be tied to such level of effort. It is far, far too late for that! We have had our chances in the past and we "blew" every one of them.

Our personal response to the state of our nation and our society should begin with the understanding that it has far more to do with *being* than with *doing*. God is looking for His people to humble themselves and repent of their sins, both personal and corporate, and put our total trust in Him. We must turn back to God as a people. It is a pre-requisite for God to heal a nation, *and His church!*

> *If My people who are called by My name humble themselves, and pray and seek My face and turn from their wicked ways, **then** I will hear from heaven and will forgive their sin and heal their land.* [25] (Emphasis Added)

A national cry such as this from God's people—with God's promised response—would change how and to what extent the things that now face us take place. While many consequences cannot be removed, and the final outcome of end-time events is fixed and certain, this author believes the pathway to that point is more open than many Christians acknowledge. ***Yes—prayer really DOES change things!*** Christians say this, but do we *really* believe it, praying fervently in the Spirit according to God's will with all our heart, expecting to see a change that God has promised if we do as He says?

We should be praying as never before! Our prayers should be for the *presence* of Almighty God to come down—not just that He "fix" things for us! We have turned our back upon *HIM—the Most High God of the Universe*—and we need to seek His presence, His mercy, His forgiveness and His healing. When we desperately seek Him in humble, genuine repentance and faith, *He will come,* and He will heal us and guide us in what He wants to do in, and through us! *Herein lies our hope!*

If you draw near to Me, I will draw near to you. (God) [26]

APPENDIX

APPENDIX I – WORLDVIEW OF THE LIBERAL, RADICAL LEFT

Those on the America-changing left—particularly the radical left—hold to a common set of *CORE WORLDVIEW BELIEFS*, with a fervently-held and inspiring *VISION FOR MANKIND*, utilizing a *MORAL CODE* to achieve their vision through a well-planned *OVER-ALL AGENDA* and methodology. Each of these key areas will be briefly considered below. While their worldview is not fully Marxist, it is more than close enough to accomplish the goal of transforming America a la Karl Marx et al.

CORE WORLDVIEW BELIEFS

The following represents the stated or assumed philosophical base regarding God, man, society and government:

1. There is no personal Creator-God, no spiritual realm and no such thing as absolute truth.
2. Humans are highly developed animals—an integral part of nature and nothing more. They are not spiritual beings made in the image of God. Apart from man's advanced level of supposed evolutionary development, there is nothing special or unique about human life, nothing to give it transcendent importance and value.
3. Man is either amoral or innately good. Mankind is not a fallen race.
4. Without the existence of God, the state becomes supreme in all things, representing the highest "good" in society, and the final authority to whom all men are accountable.
5. Society operates far more efficiently when controlled directly or indirectly by a central government. The state is better at directing the economy and ordering society than natural market and social forces under principles of liberty. The common man is considered to be incompetent at ordering his own social and economic affairs and needs government to help, or do so for him.

6. All governmental, social and environmental problems are the result of one particular "wrong" culture—Western culture, with its Christianity, Capitalism, traditional patriarchal family, and the basic assumption that man is competent to run his own life and needs the freedom to do so.

7. The smooth running of society and the solving of its problems mandates the replacement of this "wrong" culture, with a new "correct" culture, operating under a whole new political system, governed by enlightened, "politically correct" elitists, sometimes referred by its promoters as a "New World Order."

8. Nationhood is the primary cause of war. If independent national governments ceased to exist, there could be no war. The establishment of a single global governing authority is therefore essential for the survival of mankind in the nuclear age, requiring the elimination of all sovereign, independent nation-states.

   The primary target of this process is the United States of America—a world super-power recognized as the bastion of Capitalism, personal liberty, free-market prosperity, Christian values, and Western culture—the very things that all have to go.

9. The traditional family—which nurtures Christian morality, self-government, personal responsibility, patriotism and love of liberty has to be eliminated. A new model for the American family, the polar opposite of the traditional family, is to be promoted, whose non-traditional ways and practices are to be legalized, and opposition to them is to be criminalized.

VISION FOR MANKIND

The end in view is a classless, global society in which all human suffering from poverty, hunger, crime, war, class antagonism, and the avaricious destruction of the environment, etc., are eliminated.

This is a very noble-sounding vision for the "good of mankind" and has great appeal to those who are seeking something meaningful apart from themselves for which to live. This vision is a very powerful motivating tool, providing a popular humanistic alternative to Christian beliefs and values, which are considered to be intolerant and personally intrusive. This noble vision binds members of the Radical Left together as a brotherhood. It comes directly from Marxism, and motivates their cause. You catch a glimpse of the fervent bond of this "noble" cause from many Marxist web sites. Here are but two examples. In a eulogy for a fallen Communist leader, another leader said, "We pledge to carry on to complete victory of our revolution—the final triumph of the noble cause for which you lived, struggled and died." [1] At the close of an address to the people of Cuba, Fidel Castro once said, "Perhaps the endless struggle trained us for such a long battle. I think that the secret may lie in the power of a great dream, of endless enthusiasm, and of a love for our noble cause that has grown with every day of life." [2]

THE MORAL CODE

The moral code used to usher in the New World Order is very simple—the end justifies the means. Any means. In the supposed absence of absolute truth, there are no universal moral constraints to inhibit any action taken to accomplish their goals. Terms such as *justice, peace* and *moral right* have no connection to their general Christian, Western-civilization meaning. That which is just or right is simply that which advances their noble vision, no matter what it might entail. Peace refers to a state when all opposition to the noble cause and its methods is eliminated.

Their actions and methods are justified by so-called *noble lies* in which any form of lying, deception, manipulation—in fact, any atrocity that promotes their noble cause—is acceptable. If the motive is "right" nothing else matters. The idea of the noble lie is old, going back to Socrates and Plato, and has been eagerly adopted and applied by New World Order adherents.

Noble lies are the most potent and highly effective weapons in the New World Order arsenal. They are essential to bringing about the changes necessary to usher in a new, centrally controlled political and social order. People are not going to willingly give up their independence, their national identity, their way of life, their property, and their liberty. These things can only be taken from them "peacefully" by massive, consistent, blatant deception and lying. For those classes or groups upon whom this does not work, there is always "good old-fashioned" Marxist gulags and genocide. (All in a noble cause of course.)

THE OVER-ALL AGENDA

The over-all agenda of the liberal left is simply to destroy traditional values and ways of living, and replace them with totally new ones. The redefinition of the values and norms of society and the reshaping of America's culture requires both direct and indirect centralized control of all the fundamental operating functions of society. Getting this control is a long and painstaking process, but essential to fulfilling the vision.

Eventually, a globalized, New World Order under a single unified global government will be established. However, such a government can never come into being as long as there is a powerful, free, independent liberty-loving nation in the world. Therefore, the nation that has led the free world for over ninety years since America determined the outcome of WW I, has to be brought down. Americans who work to this end should not be considered as unpatriotic according to this worldview. What they are doing is for the ultimate "good" of America, and indeed the whole human race.

APPENDIX II – THE TRUE NATURE OF MARXISM/COMMUNISM

The theoretical basis of Marxism is the social, economic and political philosophy of Karl Marx and his assistant Frederick Engels which supposedly explains the source of society's problems and how society and the economy must be changed and controlled in order to solve them. Their goal was to bring every nation in the world under Marxist-Communist control—their control. They published the Communist Manifesto in 1848 to outline the process for achieving this, so there is no ideological or tactical difference between Marxism and Communism, they are one and the same thing. Communist parties can be thought of as doing the dirty-work of executing the first phase of the overall process—the destruction of Western nations, with their Capitalist, Christian culture, and the establishment of Marxist, totalitarian states. This is still the purpose and goal of Communism today.

Leaders of all Communist nations—both past and present—are in a class of their own, far different from even the most notorious of Western politicians. They got to the top by ruthless manipulation, lying, heinous cunning and the extermination of those who got in their way. They are murderers—many of them mass murderers. (Just look at the record!) They are nothing less than criminal psychopaths. They are certainly NOT humanitarians, working for the betterment of the working class and of mankind. They have murdered over one hundred million peasants and ordinary working-class people—the so-called proletariat class they claim to represent. They do not believe the social and economic nonsense that Karl Marx wrote, which is used to give a "noble" vision of a better world in the future—a vision which justifies genocide and the ruthless, barbaric acts necessary to put Communist leaders in power and keep them there.

So in actual practice, Marxism / Communism is nothing less than a monstrous process to steal absolute control of government and society through infiltration, deception, and/or straight-out Communist force and brutality. To those at the top, Communism is all about personal power. This was well described by J.R. Nyquist at a Frontpage Symposium, where he elaborated on a "remarkable explanation" of the nature of Communism given by defector General Ion Mihai Pacepa (the highest-ranking official ever to defect from the former Soviet bloc). Nyquist said:

We are confused about basic concepts, definitions—about the nature of Communism . . . [W]e should not credit Communism as an idea . . . Karl Marx did not believe in Communism. He was a cynical man who didn't believe in anything, and the same may be said of Mao and Stalin, or any of the truly effective "Communist" leaders. Karl Marx wanted to be dictator of Germany, and created his ideology for the sake of building a new kind of power—mainly for himself. He was not a humanitarian, but a would-be political murderer who failed to take office . . .

Mao said that 'Marxism-Leninism is better than a machine gun.' He did not mean that Marxism-Leninism is true. A machine gun is not truth. It is a weapon. So I say again: we should not credit Communism as an idea, but only as a weapon. Each decade after 1917 the weapon was modified according to the requirements of the moment. So flexible is this weapon, and so ready to dispense with outward labels and names, that even when people have been inoculated after living under totalitarianism, the totalitarian organism mutates and re-infects them once again. As previously indicated, this organism is not an idea but an emerging criminal class whose cynicism is as limitless as their ambition. By fixating on Communism as an idea, many of us have lost our way upon the deceptive surface of the phenomenon that continually redefines and reinvents itself. From the dictatorship of the proletariat to the state of the whole people, it is the same criminal organization at work.[1]

APPENDIX III– COLD WAR MILITARY FORCE COMPARISON

TABLE 3: COLD WAR NUCLEAR MISSILE FORCE COMPARISON

SOURCE OF DATA: The following tables have been generated from numbers taken or calculated from John Collins' work US-Soviet Military Balance 1980-1985, (pp. 167-231) with one exception.[1] Mr. Collins was at the time a Senior Specialist in National Defense at the Library of Congress whose work was considered authoritative.

| | NUCLEAR MISSILE DATA | | | | | | TOTAL STRATEGIC FORCE SUMMARY | | | | | | | |
| | | | | | | | 1975 | | | | 1980 | | | |
USA	Warhead Yield MT	No. of Warhds	Totl MT	Throw-weight, lb.	Rnge Naut. Miles	CEP Naut. Miles	Total No. of Misls	Total No. of War-heads	Total MT	Total Throw-weight, lb.	Total No. of Misls	TotalNo. of War-heads	Total MT	Total Throw-weight, lb.
ICBM TITAN 2	9	1	9.00	8,275	7,250	0.80	54	54	486	446,850	52	52	468	430,300
MINUTEMAN 2	1	1	1.00	1,625	8,000	0.34	450	450	450	731,250	450	450	450	731,250
---3 MK12	0.17	3	0.51	1,975	8,000	0.12	550	1,650	281	1,086,250	473	1,419	241	934,175
---3 MK12A	0.34	3	1.02	1,975	8,000	0.12					77	231	79	152,075
TOTAL ICBM							1,054	2,154	1,217	2,264,350	1,052	2,152	1,238	2,247,800
SLBM POLARIS A2	0.8	1	0.80	1,400	1,500	0.50	32	32	26	44,800				
POLARIS A3	0.2	3	0.60	1600	2,500	0.50	176	528	106	281,600	80	240	48	128,000
POSEIDON C3	0.04	10	0.40	1900	2,500	0.25	448	4,480	179	851,200	416	4,160	166	790,400
TRIDENT 1	0.1	8	0.80	3000	4,000	0.25					80	640	64	240,000
TOTAL SLBM							656	5,040	310	1,177,600	576	5,040	278	1,158,400
GRAND TOTAL							1,710	7,194	1,527	3,441,950	1,628	7,192	1,516	3,406,200

SOVIET UNION

			5.00	4,000	6,500	1.50	190	190	950	760,000				
ICBM SS-7	5	1	5.00	4,000	6,500	1.50	190	190	950	760,000	640	640	838	1,600,000
SS-8	4	1	4.00	3,500	6,900	1.00	19	19	76	66,500	60	60	36	78,000
SS-9	25	1	25.00	11,000	7,000	0.40	298	298	7,450	2,400,000	130	520	390	783,250
SS-11	1.31	1	1.31	2,500	5,500	0.60	960	960	1,258	78,000	20	20	120	120,000
SS-13	0.6	1	0.60	1,300	6,000	1.00	60	40	36	60,250	26	26	624	390,000
SS-17 MOD 1	0.75	4	3.00	6,025	5,500	0.24	10	10	30		162	1,296	2,592	2,705,400
SS-17 MOD 2	6	1	6.00	6,000	5,700	0.23								
SS-18 MOD 1	24	8	24.00	15,000	6,000	0.23	10	360	240	150,000	120	1,200	600	2,004,000
SS-18 MOD 2	2	10	16.00	16,700	6,000	0.23					180	1,080	594	1,354,500
SS-18 MOD 4	0.5	6	5.00	16,700	5,500	0.14								
SS-19 MOD 1	0.55	1	3.30	7,525	5,000	0.19	60	60	198	451,500	40	40	400	280,000
SS-19 MOD 2	10	6	10.00	7,000	5,500	0.16								
SS-19 MOD 3	0.55		3.30	7,500	5,500	0.13					20	120	66	150,000
TOTAL ICBM							1,607	1,937	10,238	3,966,250	1,398	5,002	6,260	9,465,150
SLBM SS-N-4	1	1	1.00	2600	300	1.50	21	21	21	54,600	57	57	114	148,200
SS-N-5 ?	2	1	2.00	2600	900	1.50								
SS-N-6	1	1	1.00	2200	1,600	0.70	60	60	120	156,000	468	468	468	1,029,600
SS-N-8	1	1	1.00	2400	4,800	0.80	528	528	528	1,161,600	292	292	292	700,800
SS-N-17	1	1	1.00	3600	2,000	0.75					12	12	12	43,200
SS-N-18 MOD 3	1	3	3.00	3600	4,500	0.50	156	156	156	374,400	160	480	480	576,000
TOTAL SLBM							765	765	825	1,746,600	989	1,309	1,366	2,497,800
GRAND TOTAL							2,372	2,702	11,063	5,712,850	2,387	6,311	7,626	11,962,950

TABLE 4: COLD WAR STRATEGIC FORCE COMPARISON

	1975	1980
STRATEGIC DEFENSE		
ABM, SAM LAUNCHERS		
USA	108	0
SOVIET UNION	9,500	9,300
INTERCEPTOR AIRCRAFT		
USA	371	269
SOVIET UNION	2,600	2,550
TACTICAL DEFENSE		
A/A GUNS		
USA	1,770	3,520
SOVIET UNION	10,500	9,500
SAM LAUNCHERS		
USA	1,080	1,185
SOVIET UNION	1,770	3,520
ACTIVE MILITARY PERSONNEL		
USA	2,123,000	2,094,000
SOVIET UNION	4,763,000	4,837,000
READY RESERVE PERSONNEL		
USA	1,526,000	1,259,000
SOVIET UNION	8,570,000	9,149,000
GROUND FORCE DIVISIONS		
USA	22	24
SOVIET UNION	174	185
HEAVY AND MEDIUM BATTLE TANKS		
USA	8,223	10,985
SOVIET UNION	44,050	48,000
HEAVY ARTILLERY		
USA	4,234	4,149
SOVIET UNION	13,900	19,300
TACTICAL AIRCRAFT		
USA	2,816	2938
SOVIET UNION	4,375	4375
AIRCRAFT CARRIERS		
USA	15	12
SOVIET UNION	0	0

NOMENCLATURE

A/A	Anti-Aircraft (gun)
ABM	Anti-Ballistic Missile
Deployed	In active service, ready for immediate use
ICBM	Inter-Continental Ballistic Missile
SLBM	Submarine-Launched Ballistic Missile
Throw-weight	The total pay-load of a missile– the weight of its weapons system.
CEP	Circular Error Probability. A measure of missile accuracy—the radius of a target which the missile has a 50 percent chance of hitting.
MT	(Megatonnage) The measure of a nuclear warhead yield in terms of the equivalent blast force of a million tons of conventional high explosive.
Nautical Mile	An international unit for air and sea travel. 1.1508 British miles.
Strategic Forces	Those forces used against the national resources of an enemy– striking the source of their military, economic and political power
Tactical Forces	Those forces used in battle against opposing military forces.

BIBLIOGRAPHY

Beichman, Arnold. *Roosevelt's Failure at Yalta, Hoover Institution Digest,* October 30, 2004.

Bowers, Dr. James. *Communist Encirclement.* 1990s Summit Lecture Series. Summit Ministries, Manitou Springs, Co.

- - - *Humanism in Action, Conclusion.*

- - - *Humanism in the 60's.*

- - - *Humanism in the 70's.*

- - - *America's War in Vietnam.*

Bowers, Clark. *Is Communism Really Dead?* 1990s Summit Lecture Series. Summit Ministries, Manitou Springs, Co.

Buchanan, Patrick J. *The Death of the West,* Thomas Dunne, 2002.

Collins, John M. (Senior Specialist in National Defense, Library of Congress), *U.S.-Soviet Military Balance: Concepts and Capabilities, 1960-1980,* McGraw-Hill, 1980.

Graham, Lt. Gen. Daniel O. *Shall America Be Defended.* Arlington House, 1979.

Keegan, Maj. Gen. George. "New Assessment Put on Soviet Threat." *Aviation Week and Space Technology,* March 28, 1977, p. 40. http://archive.aviationweek.com/issue/19770328

Kimball, Roger, *The Long March.* Encounter Books, 2000.

Nyquist, J. R. "Is there a defense against nuclear attack?" *WorldNetDaily,* November 1, 1999.

Pipes, Richard. *Why the Soviet Union Thinks It Could Fight and Win a Nuclear War, Commentary,* July 1977, p. 34.

- - - *Nuclear Weapons Policy Questioned, Aviation Week and Space Technology,* November 6, 1978

Schlafly, Phyllis, Chester Ward. *Kissinger on the Couch.*1975, Arlington House.

- - - *The Gravediggers.* Pere Marquette Press. 1964.

- - - *The Betrayers.* Pere Marquette Press. 1968.

Skousen, W. Cleon. *The Naked Communist.* Ensign. 9th Edition, 1961.

Stormer, John A. *None Dare Call It Treason . . . 25 Years Later.* Liberty Bell, 1990.

Sutton, Antony. *The Best Enemy Money Can Buy.* Liberty House Press, 1968.

- - - *Western Technology and Soviet Economic Development 1945 to 1965.* Hoover Institution Press, Stanford University, Stanford, Ca. 1973.

Walt, Gen. Lewis W. *The Eleventh Hour.* Caroline House. 1979.

END NOTES

PREFACE

1. According to Lt. Gen. Ion .M. Pacepa, the highest official ever to have defected from the former Soviet block, speaking in Jamie Glazov's book, *High Noon for America,* Mantura Books, 2012. p. 55.

CHAPTER 1

1. Thomas J. DiLorenzo, *How Capitalism Saved America* by (2005), p. 194. Jim Powell. *FDR's Folly,* 2003, pp.15-17.
2. Arnold Beichman, "Roosevelt's Failure at Yalta," *Hoover Institution Digest,* quoted in Charles Bohlen's memoirs.
3. George Kennan, "Russia and the West Under Lenin and Stalin" (Boston: Little., Brown, 1960), quoted in Beichman
4. William C. Bullitt, "How We Won the War and Lost the Peace," Life, 30 August 1948, p. 94. Quoted in CIA Library, "How 'Uncle Joe' Bugged FDR."
5. Yalta Conference. Wikipedia
6. *The Des Moines Register,* Des Moines Iowa. Sunday, February 8, 1948, p. 6.
7. M. Stanton Evans, "McCarthyism--Waging the Cold War in America." *Human Events,* May 30, 1997.
8. Tom Winter and Allan Ryskind, "M. Stanton Evans Reveals the Truth about McCarthy," *Human Events,* Nov. 19, 2007.
9. M. Stanton Evans, "McCarthyism: Waging the Cold War in America," *Human Events,* May 30 1997.
10. Ibid.
11. Ibid.
12. Jon Basil Utley, "Communism - McCarthy Was Right" © 2000 *WorldNetDaily.com*
13. Ibid.

CHAPTER 2

1. Walt, *Eleventh Hour* p. 39.
2. James Bowers, *Humanism in the 70s.*
3. James Bowers, *Communist Encirclement.*
4. Anne W. Carroll, "Who Lost China?" Global Catholic Network website, http://www.ewtn.com/library/homelibr/fr89102.txt
5. Forrest C. Pogue, *George C. Marshall, Statesman, 1945-1959,* Viking Adult, 1987, pp. 65-66. Quoted in Anne W. Carroll.
6. Tang Tsou, *America's Failure in China, 1941-1945,* U. of Chicago, 1964, p. 356. Quoted in Anne W. Carroll.
7. Ibid. p. 364.
8. "Military Situation in the Far East" Hearings before the Committee on Armed Services and the Committee on Foreign Relations, US Senate, 82nd Congress (Washington, 1951), p. 377. Quoted in Anne W. Carroll.
9. Tom Winter and Allan Ryskind, "M. Stanton Evans Reveals the Truth." *Human Events,* Nov. 19, 2007
10. James Bowers, *Communist Encirclement.*
11. James Bowers, *Communist Encirclement* and *Humanism in the 70s.*
12. Ronald Reagan speech to the National Association of Evangelicals in Orlando, Florida, March 8, 1983.
13. Lawrence W. Reed, "Grenada, 20 Years Later," *National Review On Line,* http://www.nationalreview.com/comment/reed200310240950.asp

CHAPTER 3

1. Melvin Laird, *A House Divided—America's Strategy Gap.* Regnery, 1962. Quoted in Schlafly and Ward, *Kissinger* pp. 23-24.
2. Keegan, *New Assessment,* p. 40. Pipes, *Why the Soviet Union Thinks,* p. 34.
3. Pipes, *Nuclear Weapons Policy.*
4. Nyquist, *Is there a Defense.*
5. Ibid.
6. Lenin V.I., *Selected Works,* Vol IX, p. 477. Quoted in Skousen, *Naked Communist,* p. 304.
7. Skousen, pp. 304, 305.
8. Stalin, Joseph, *The Great Patriotic War of the Soviet Union,* Moscow, 1946, p. 55. Quoted in Skousen, p. 308.
9. Nyquist, *Is there a Defense.*

10. Keegan, *New Assessment*, p. 42.
11. Based on the testimony of a Soviet military student who later broke away from the Communist Party. He was quoting Dimitri L. Manuilski, who later served as Russia's UN delegate. Quoted in Stormer, *None Dare Call*, p. 1, 92.

CHAPTER 4

1. *Commentary* Magazine July 1, 1977.
2. Lt. Gen. Daniel O. Graham (Once Director of the Defense Intelligence Agency and Deputy Director of the CIA), *The Emerging Strategic Imbalance*. ACU Education and Research Institute, January 1977 p. 24.
3. Pipes, *Why the Soviet Union Thinks*.
4. Walt, *Eleventh Hour*, pp. 47-48.
5. Arthur Schlesinger Jr., "Partisan Review, May– June 1947," reprinted, Congressional record February 6, 1962. Quoted in Stormer, p. 188.
6. Dean Rusk, Speech given at World Affairs Conference, International Union of Electrical, Radio, and Machine Workers, Washington DC, February 25, 1964. Quoted in Stormer, p. 253.
7. Hearings, Military Cold War Education and Speech Review Policies, Senate Armed Services Committee, June 4, 1962, Part six, page 2805. Quoted in Stormer p. 93.
8. *The Chicago Tribune* June 17, 1962. Quoted in Stormer p. 93.
9. State of the Union Message, Jan. 13, 1967. Quoted in Stormer, p. 256.
10. Strobe Talbott, "The Birth of the Global Nation," *Time Magazine* July 20, 1992 p. 70.

CHAPTER 5

1. US Department of State, <www.state.gov/r/pa/ho/time/cwr/17601pf.htm>
2. *St. Louis Post-Dispatch*, November 28, 1961. Quoted in Stormer, *None Dare Call*, p. 267.
3. *Chicago Tribune*, June 18, 1962. Quoted in Stormer p. 92.
4. John D. Lofton Jr, "Don't Trust the Soviets," *Conservative Digest*, Sept. 1978.

5. Dept. of State Publication 7277—*Freedom From War* (US Government Printing Office: 1961 O---609147 can be seen on <http://www.mikenew.com/pub7277.html

6. From US Dept. of State document 7277, September 1961, pp. 5-6.

7. Sen. John Tower, Congressional Record, January 29, 1962. Quoted in Stormer page p. 87.

8. Sen. Joseph Clark, Congressional Record, March 1, 1962, page 2936. Quoted in Stormer p. 87.

9. Arms-Control and Disarmament Act, September 26, 1961, Section 2 a, b, c. Stormer p. 87. Details given in BLUEPRINT FOR THE PEACE RACE – Outline of Basic Provisions of a Treaty on General and Complete Disarmament in a Peaceful World. UNITED STATES ARMS CONTROL AND DISARMAMENT AGENCY PUBLICATION 4. General Series 3, Released May 1962.

10. Schlafly and Ward, *Gravediggers*, p. 55-6.

11. Schlafly and Ward, *Betrayers*, p. 59.

12. Ibid. p. 60.

13. Ibid. pp. 59-60.

14. Schlafly and Ward, *Gravediggers*, p. 15.

15. Schlafly and Ward, *Betrayers,* pp. 56-57.

16. Ibid. pp. 58-59.

17. Schlafly and Ward, *Gravediggers* p. 16.

18. Ibid.

19. *St. Louis Grove Democrat* March 3, 1963. Quoted in Stormer, p. 88.

20. *St. Louis Post-Dispatch*, March 28, 1963. Quoted in Stormer, p. 88.

21. Ibid. Dec. 18-19, 1963. Quoted in Stormer, *None Dare Call*, p. 88.

22. Schlafly and Ward, *Gravediggers*, p. 15.

23. Ibid. p. 15.

24. Ibid. pp. 15-16.

25. *New York Times* November 16, 1961: *Saturday Evening Post*, June 23, 1963. Quoted in Stormer, p. 89

26. *Human Events*, August 10, 1963. Quoted in Stormer, p. 89.

27. From figures compiled from various official and non-official sources by Wm. Robert Johnston, a physics doctoral candidate at the University of Texas. <www.johnstonsarchive.net/nuclear/nucstock-1.html>

28. Keith B. Payne, Dr., at The United States Senate Committee on Foreign Relations hearing on: "US Strategic and Arms Control

Objectives;" May 5, 1999. Dr. Payne's testimony given on <http://www.nipp.org/Adobe/testimony%205_99.pdf>

29. Walt, *Eleventh Hour*, pp. 3-4.

30. "Military Implications of the Treaty on the Limitation of anti-Ballistic Missile Systems and the Interim Agreement on Limitation of Strategic Offensive Weapons." Hearing before the "Committee on Armed Forces, United States Senate, 92nd Congress, 2nd Session" (Washington, D.C.: US, GPO, 1972). p. 121

31. Keegan, *New Assessment*, p. 46.

32. Press Conferences in Moscow, May 26, 27, 1972. Quoted in Schlafly and Ward. *Kissinger*, pp. 502-03.

33. Schlafly and Ward. *Kissinger*, pp. 508-09.

34. Ibid. p. 504.

35. *US News and World Report*, July 18, 1977.

36. Schlafly and Ward, *Kissinger*, p. 687.

37. "Department of Defense Report, FY 1975," March 4, 1975, p.72. As quoted in Schlafly and Ward, *Kissinger*, p 687.

38. Schlafly and Ward. *Kissinger*, pp. 687-88.

39. *Human Events*, August 3, 1985. Quoted in Stormer, p. 250.

40. *Washington Times*, July 30, 1987. Quoted in Stormer, p. 245-246.

41. Evans, M. Stanton, "It's no wonder we are losing," *The Hour - Norwalk Ct.*, Commentary, July 25, 1985.

42. *Human Events*, August 3, 1985. Quoted in Stormer *None Dare Call*, p. 246.

43. Walt, *Eleventh Hour*, pp. 53-4.

44. The information in this section is summarized from Antony Sutton's comprehensive books, Sutton was a Research Fellow at the Hoover Institution for War, Revolution and Peace, at Stanford, California from 1968 to 1973, where he produced a monumental three volume study, Western Technology and Soviet Economic Development. He had access to information not available to most researchers outside establishment circles.

45. Sutton, *The Best Enemy*, Appendix III

46. Ibid. Ch. 12.

47. Ibid. Ch. 6.

48. Ibid. Ch. 29.

49. Ibid. Ch. 2, 3.

50. Ibid. Ch. 7.

51. Ibid. Ch. 5.

CHAPTER 6

1. Walt, *Eleventh Hour*, p. 33.
2. Ibid. p. 4.
3. Ibid. p. 35.
4. *US News and World Report*, February 14, 1966.
5. *St. Louis Globe Democrat*, Jan 27, 1967. Quoted in Stormer, p. 235.
6. *US News and World Report*, February 14, 1966.
7. *The St. Globe Democrat*. May 13, 1967. Quoted in Stormer, p. 236.
8. Ibid. January 27, 1967. Quoted in Stormer, p. 234.
9. Ibid. June 13, 1972. Quoted in Stormer, p. 236.
10. Ibid. Sept. 13, 1967. Quoted in Stormer, p. 234.
11. Ibid. Sept 15, 1967. Quoted in Stormer, p.234
12. Bowers, James, *America's War in Vietnam.*
13. Ibid.
14. Ibid.
15. Ibid.
16. Allan Brownfield. "How Media Bias Distorts our View of the World." Quoted in Stormer, p. 238.
17. *New York Review of Books,* article, quoting AIM (Accuracy in Media) report, April 1983. Quoted in Stormer, p. 240.
18. Walt, *Eleventh Hour*, pp. 69-70.
19. Norman Podhoretz, "Why We Were in Vietnam" p. 125, Quoted in Stormer, p. 240.
20. *Daily World*, December 28, 1973. Quoted in Stormer, p. 238.
21. Bowers, James, *America's War in Vietnam.*
22. Ibid.
23. *1995 Information Please Almanac Atlas & Yearbook* 49th edition, Houghton Mifflin Company, Boston & New York 1996, pp. 117, 161, 292.
24. Bowers, James, *America's War in Vietnam.*
25. Address to the Nation Announcing Conclusion of an Agreement on Ending the War and Restoring Peace in Vietnam. January 23, 1973.

CHAPTER 7

1. Graham, *Shall America*, p. 15; and Kozicharow, Eugene, "Nuclear Attack Survival Aspects Studied," *Aviation Week & Space Technology*, Nov. 14, 1977; and Joanne S. Gailar, Joanne S., and Wigner, Eugene, P., "Civil Defense in the US," *Forsight,* May-June, 1974; Jones, T.K.,

and Edwards, M.R., *Deterrence and Civil Defense*, ACU Education and Research Institute

2. Advertisement in *New York Times* and other papers across the nation, January 21, 1979. The full text can be seen on <http://www.workers. org/marcy/generals/chap7.html>

3. Tyrrell, R. Emmett Jr., "Such Good Friends," *New York Times,* June 18, 1977

4. John R. Coyne Jr., *The Word is Freedom*; An exclusive interview with Vladimir Bukocsky, Russian political prisoner and exile. *National Review*, April 1, 1977, pp. 378-82.

CHAPTER 8

1. Ronald Reagan speech, March 8, 1983, to a meeting of the National Association of Evangelicals in Orlando, Florida.

2. *The New York Times*, October 7, 1986.

3. Reagan speech, June 12, 1987. The History Place, Great Speech Collections.   http://www.historyplace.com/speeches/reagan-tear-down.htm

4. Douglas Brinkley, "A Clarion Call for Freedom," October 30, 1999. *Hoover Digest*, 1999 No.   4. <http://www.hoover.org/research/ clarion-call-freedom>

5. J. R. Nyquist, "Russia's Long-range Vision," *WorldNetDaily*, June 19, 2000.

6. Anatoliy Golitsyn, *New Lies for Old*, Gsg and Assoc., 1990, pp. 327-28.

7. Anatoliy Golitsyn, *Perestroika Deception,* Edward Harle, 1995, p. 87.

8. Mikhail Gorbachev, *Perestroika: New Thinking for Our Country and the World,* HarperCollins, 1987, p. 36.

9. Stormer, p. 6-7.

10. *The Gainesville Sun*, December 29, 1991

CHAPTER 9

1. ARPA-IDA Study Memo No. 7, March 10, 1962, State Department Contract SCC 28270, February 24, 1961. Quoted in Schlafly, *The Gravediggers*, p. 78.

2. Schlafly and Ward, *The Betrayers*, Schlafly, p. 16.

CHAPTER 10

1. Buchanan, pp. 75-79, 81, 86.
2. Charles A. Reich, The Greening of America, Bantam Books, 1971, p. 2. Quoted in Buchanan, p. 77
3. Most of the information in the following portion of this section is condensed from Kimble
4. Kimball, p. 7.
5. Quoted in Kimball, pp. 15-16.
6. Kimball, pp. 11-12, 14, 18.
7. Ibid. p. 23.
8. Ibid. p. 107.
9. Ibid. pp. 104-05.
10. Ibid.
11. Ibid. pp. 112-113.
12. Ibid. pp. 116-117.
13. Ibid. pp. 117-118.
14. Ibid. p. 119.
15. Ibid. pp. 274-75.

CHAPTER 11

1. George Weigel, "Rediscovering the Martyrology." First Things. http://www.firstthings.com/web-exclusives/2014/02/rediscovering-the-martyrology
2. Usually attributed to Blaise Pascal, although it has not be found in his writings, which does not in any way detract from the truth of the statement.
3. Carpenter, Edmond James. The Mayflower Pilgrims, Abington Press, 1918, pp. 98-99. Reprinted by Christian Liberty Press, 1993.
4. Luke 9:62. NASB
5. Verna Hall, The Christian History of the Constitution of the United States of America - Christian Self Government. . Foundation for American Christian Education. 1960. pp. 271-272. (In quoting John Fisk's "Civil Government in the United States" - 1890)
6. Leviticus 19:15. NASB
7. Leviticus 19:9-10. NASB. (Also Leviticus 23:22; Deuteronomy 24:19-21).
8. Noted by Justice Hugo Black in Torcasso v. Watkins, 1961.

9. Shelby Sharpe, "Theology and Law,"– Understanding the Times lecture video, Summit Ministries, CO.

10. Roscoe Pound, *Law and Morals* (2d ed. Chapel Hill, 1926), Lecture I, "The Historical View." pp. 12-14. Quoted on http://www.constitution.org/haines/haines_012.htm#012-004.

11. "Russia and NATO 'actively preparing for war," *Washington Times*, August 12, 2015. "Russian General Seeks Nuclear First-Strike Option Against US" *Fox News*, Sept 4, 2014 "Russia Building Dozens of Underground Nuclear Command Bunkers" *Newsmax*, August 25, 2016

12. J. R. Nyquist, describing what Lee's book reveals.

13. "Russia's anti-American fever goes beyond the Soviet era." *Washington Post*, March 8 2015.

14. "China Preparing For Future Fight With US," *CNN*, June 2003.

15. "Washington Is Preparing for a Long War with China," *US News and World Report*. March 31 2011; "Revealed: America's Backup Plan in Case of War with China," *The National Interest*. Feb. 25 2016.

16. "China, Russia Planning Space Attacks on US Satellites," Bill Gertz, *Washington Times*. March 16, 2016.

17. "Disarm Now, Ask Questions Later: Obama's Nuclear Weapons Policy" The Heritage Foundation, Backgrounder #2826 on National Security and Defense, July 12, 2013

18. "Army details how it will cut to its smallest size since before World War II," Dan Lamothe *Washington Post*, July 9, 2015.

19. "Fox: Drastic Budget Cuts Taking Harsh Toll on Air Force." *Newsmax*. May 14, 2016. "US Navy Absorbing $7 Billion Budget Cut." *DefenseNews*, Feb. 10, 2016

20. Luke 12:48. NASB

21. Galatians 6:7. NASB.

22. Jeremiah 4:22 NASB.

23. Sandoz, Ellis, ed. *Political Sermons of the Founding Era*. Liberty Fund, 1991, 2nd ed. (1779 pages of political sermons.)

24. To read some of their story, see "Killing Christians" by Tom Doyle, 2015

25. 2 Chronicles 7:14 ESV.

26. From James 4:8; Zecheriah. 1:3; Malachi. 3:7.

APPENDIX I

1. From: *African Communist*, No. 51, fourth Quarter, 1972. <http://www.sacp.org.za/docs/history/dadoo-33.html>
2. From an article in the Daily online newspaper of the Communist Party of Canada of March 2003. <http://www.cpcml.a/tmld.ca/tmld/D33048.htm>

APPENDIX II

1. Glazov, *High Noon for America. The Coming Showdown*, Mantua Books. 2012, p. 60-61.

APPENDIX III

1. The 1400 lb. throw weight for the SLBM POLARIS A2 has been estimated from undocumented data provided by contributors from various universities and policy analysis institutions compiled by the Claremont Institute <http://www.claremont.org/> on their missile threat project website. <http://missilethreat.com/>

CPSIA information can be obtained
at www.ICGtesting.com
Printed in the USA
LVOW11s1933180917
549114LV00001B/104/P